GAY CONVERSATIONS
With Nello Pozzobon

Hope for the Homosexual

By Lynda Allison Doty

Gay Conversations

By Lynda Allison Doty

© Copyright 2002 by Lynda Allison Doty

Unless contained within quoted material, or otherwise noted, all Scriptures are from the King James Version (KJV).

Published by:

AWP Ministries
P.O. Box 292100
Sacramento, CA 95829
Director@awpministries.org
ladawp@aol.com

WARNING: THE MATERIAL IN THIS BOOK IS INTENDED FOR ADULTS AND MATURE TEENAGERS. HOWEVER, THIS IS A SUBJECT THAT PARENTS SHOULD PLAN TO DISCUSS WITH THEIR CHILDREN.

ISBN: 0-9719852-3-5

Printed in the United States by:
Morris Publishing
3212 East Highway 30
Kearney, NE 68847
1-800-650-7888

Table of Contents

Thanksgiving

This book would not have been possible without Nello Pozzobon. He has poured his heart into what he considers a labour of love. I want to give him my heartfelt thanks. I have come to love this brother in the Lord. He is special to me, very humble, and very precious.

And thanks go again to my awesome husband. Oh how I love him! He is my most loyal "fan," and supports me in all that I do. Never once did he tell me not to write this book. He always says the same thing: "If the Lord says do it, honey, you'd better do it. Go for it!" Thank you, darling, for believing in me!

And my deepest thanks of all to my Lord and Savior, Jesus Christ, for the work He is doing in my son Joseph Stephen's heart and life.

Foreword

While working for a large insurance company in the early 1970's, our district sales manager would often spout a cliché in his efforts to stimulate sales. His statement, "Everyone wants progress, no one wants change," has remained with me to this day. As agents came to him for new and innovative ideas to close contracts, he understood that more than likely these salesmen would revert to their old ways and never try something that was outside their realm. In his business wisdom, he realized that unless people were willing to change, progress would never materialize. We all could expect the same old results.

Our relationship with The Savior is predicated on change. "Ye must be born again" (John 3:7.) and "Therefore if any man be in Christ, he is a new creature: old things are passed away; behold, all things are become new" (2Cor5:17) remind us not only of our conversion experience but also of our experiences along the way. Without change we cannot "go on to perfection" (Heb 6:1). How frustrated the Lord must be with us when we choose the old road, when He is trying to lead us on a new path!

This book is about change. In *Gay Conversations*, Sister Doty challenges every reader to allow change to take place. To the homosexual, the moving of God's Spirit in one's life *will* bring about change. Change of thought pattern, change of lifestyle, change of outlook and finally a change of destination. As Brother Nello Pozzobon's pastor, I have witnessed a wonderful miracle unfold before my eyes. He has allowed the Lord to chink away at the old man and shape the new. But just as important, Sister Doty challenges the Church to change. Preconceived ideas, and "this is the way it has always been," must become part of the past. I must confess, I was there... my opinion, my thoughts.... then Brother Nello!

In these last days the Lord is drawing people from depths of sin unheard of just a few short years ago. "But evil men and seducers shall wax worse and worse, deceiving, and being deceived" (2 Tim 3:13). The Church has an opportunity to position herself to reap the souls that are involved in all manner of sin. In the name of Jesus, let it be so!

Stephen Mathias, Pastor
The Lighthouse of Cape Cod UPC

1

Heart to Heart

This book is written to three different groups: to the gay person, to the Church, and to those who love the homosexual. One pastor told me, "I am really interested in your new book on homosexuality. But I would like to see a book which goes beyond 'pat' answers and actually provides direction for people to extricate themselves, with God's help, from this debilitating sin." I believe this book can help accomplish that goal, because there are no pat answers. I found out while researching this book, there aren't even any pat questions!

I did not seek to write this book—in fact, I fought it. There were fears pertaining to pride that had to be dealt with at once. And then the feeling of inadequacy to tackle this kind of project. Also, all the signs were leading to the knowledge that I would have to release some skeletons from my own closet, because this kind of work can only be done with an open and honest heart. It always hurts when you cut a vein.

I have lain awake many nights, crying for those lost in the sin of homosexuality. Crying out to God to deliver and to save and to heal. Crying out for God to send someone to these people. And then, one night, He whispered to me, "Go." And I asked, "Why me?" And He asked, "Why not you?"

"I am not homosexual, Lord."

"But you love them."

We win people by loving them to God. Grace and Mercy always precede Judgment. Grace and Mercy can crack the hardest heart and win the darkest soul. Much healing is required, and only God can heal. That is why the homosexual's answer lies in God. They need to know about the love of God, and then to experience that love. Many homosexuals don't know what real love is. They have searched a lifetime for an elusive feeling that does not exist, or for the tenderness of a dad who was never there.

Please realize that I am not dishing out "sloppy-agape" here. This book deals with truth, and it calls sin, sin. It also deals with lies— lies from the pit of hell designed to destroy the family, the church, and the individual soul. Gays have already heard how bad they are—and most of all, they have heard it from themselves. Much anguish has been felt in the deep of the night—many pillows soaked with tears of remorse and hopelessness. While the rest of the city slept, they were fighting their demons. Yes, they have already told themselves how bad they are, so I don't believe that is my job here.

There are enough books already with the message that crushes and destroys any spark of hope that might be left. When they start hearing that message again, the walls go up, the ears are plugged, and you can preach until you drop from exhaustion, and nothing will happen. In the words of Professor Higgins, "They listen very nicely, then go out and do precisely what they like."

What *will* open the doors to these hearts is the message of hope. There are countless homosexuals wanting to hear from someone that they can be set free. They want to know God's real love. Don't believe the lie that homosexuals are happy, or gay, in their sin and don't want to change. Many of them do not, but let's reach for those who do. Let's seek them out.

It is my prayer that you will feel my heartbeat, and know that I am real. God has poured His love for you into this earthen vessel. The love I feel for you is not of myself, but of Him. Some of you have prayed for God to reveal His love for you. Consider that a prayer answered, for He is loving you now, through me, and through Nello.

So, who is Nello? We will get into some of his testimony in a minute. For now, it is enough to know that Nello is a man who lived deep in the homosexual lifestyle for many years—and God delivered him! Now God has delivered countless homosexuals in our ranks. What makes Nello unique is that he has chosen to stand up and give the word of his testimony. Nello has a heart that longs to reach out to those embroiled in the hurt and pain of homosexuality. To this end, he helped me to see the immediate need for this book, and supplied me with much material.

Nello has been open and honest with me throughout the process of getting this material into print. He is a man with a tremendous sense of humor; I absolutely enjoy him! He does not judge or condemn. He simply loves—or rather, allows God to love through him. Throughout the book, a lot of his material is presented as "conversations" between him and me.

There appears to be some excellent Christian-based programs out there in what's often called "ex-gay ministry." Some of them— Exodus, in particular—are doing a good work. Although the media does their utmost to suppress it, countless people are being set free from homosexual bondage. So why another book—another ministry—about homosexuality? Because there is a distinct group of people who believe that our God is One. In the Old Testament, Deuteronomy 6:4 tells us, *"Hear, O Israel: The LORD our God is one LORD."* Jesus repeats this in Mark 12:29. This book is written for them.

This group of people also believes that, according to Acts 1:8, we must have the power of the Holy Ghost residing within us. It is that power that releases and delivers and overcomes. On the birthday of the Church, heartsick men cried out to Peter and the other apostles: *"Men and brethren, what shall we do?"* Peter replied, giving them the answer for their own salvation: *"...Repent, and be baptized every one of you in the name of Jesus Christ for the remission of sins, and ye shall receive the gift of the Holy Ghost."* (Acts 2:38) (When I was Roman Catholic, we were taught that the apostle Peter was the first pope. How awesome that his message was that of Acts 2:38! If there are any Catholics reading this, please check out Peter's first message to the Church.)

Tying all these scriptural admonitions together, we see that we need, first of all, to repent. Then our vessels are clean, and the Holy Spirit can come to live inside of us. Our sins have been forgiven, and we need to have them remitted, or washed away, in the waters of baptism. When the life-giving name of Jesus is applied in baptism, as Peter instructed, it cleanses us from all sin.

For those who feel that these admonitions applied only to the original apostles, we learn in Acts 2:39 that *"...the promise is unto you, and to your children, and to all that are afar off, even as many as the Lord our God shall call."* This promise is, therefore, to everyone reading these words. If you have not had this experience, it is my prayer that you will search the Scriptures and ask God to lead you into all truth.

Missing in Action

There are those who have embraced this truth and no longer walk with God. They are called "backsliders." Although this is a biblical term, I have never been quite comfortable with it. Recently, I heard someone use the term MIA—"Missing in Action." I like that! It is so appropriate! These people are still our brothers and sisters; they just aren't fighting on the front lines anymore. They are casualties...missing in action. So, in this book, I will be calling them MIAs.

Another thing that bothers me is the fact that some church folks, when referring to MIAs, refrain from calling them their "Brother" or "Sister." I have a blood brother who is buried at Crescent Memorial Gardens in South Carolina. Although he is dead, he will always be my brother. The prodigal son was still his brother's brother, and his father's son. Let's not alienate our MIAs even further by disowning them when they need us the most!

A Note on the Use of the Word "Gay"

People in my age bracket remember when the word "gay" meant something entirely different. I really do not know when homosexuals began to use this word. I do know that in the depths of their hearts, they do not feel the gaiety and happiness indicated by the original meaning of the word. I use the word in this book because I want the homosexual to relate to me, and I to him or her. I want to meet them on their turf.

It is true that not all homosexuals want to be helped. There will always be the headliners—the militants—the abusers—and those lost in the deepest pits of evil. But there is a growing number who *do* want help. And as our world grows more perilous and fierce, we will see even more of them searching for the security of the arms of Jesus. One does not stand in the middle of an earthquake without seeking shelter. What a mission field! And I believe it is our job, mandated by the Lord Jesus, to take the Gospel to them, also. We must take the message that Christ forgives and is a God of love and compassion and understanding. Homosexuality is *not* the unpardonable sin. God can and will forgive it. He will not turn away anyone who comes to Him with a soft and repentant heart! It is our job to tell this to the homosexuals, and to tell it in a loving and compassionate way.

One of Satan's lies is that, since God is a God of love, He accepts them just as they are, so they don't have to change. Otherwise, say they, it could not be said that He loves them. We need to get this message across: Yes! God loves you! Just as you are! But—He loves you far too much to let you remain in a destructive lifestyle. He has a far better plan for you!

But for the grace of God, there go I...

2

Words to the Gay Man or Woman

As far as I am concerned, the single most important issue you will ever have to face is that of Hope. Without hope, no one will ever take the next step. And too many of you have lost hope that you can ever change. You have no hope at all that God can change your desires. The media have fed it to you gradually, one sound bite at a time, over a long period of time. It's called "conditioning." That is a psychology term, but also a marketing term. Don't take offense, but you have been conditioned to believe you have to live this way forever. You have been duped. You have become convinced that you were born this way; consequently, there's no way out. Maybe at the start, as you began to flirt with this lifestyle—to try it out, so to speak—you felt you would be able to come out of it any time you wanted. Then you found you could not. So you fell into the lie: there's nothing you can do about it, so you might as well relax and enjoy it.

At first, it was a relief to think you were born that way, because it alleviated your guilt. After all, if you were born that way, you aren't responsible; so God certainly doesn't hold you accountable. But now things are different. You discovered that this kind of life has left you full of pain, and after trying to extricate yourself, you discovered that you were bound. But you *can* change! Nello has been there, and he knows you can. There will be other testimonies in this book, all pointing to the fact that you can.

God changed all of us who are living for Him today. We have all been transformed. In fact, we have become "new creatures." II Corinthians 5:17 tells us, *"Therefore if any man be in Christ, he is a new creature: old things are passed away; behold, all things are become new."* Did you know that this actually means we have become a new "species?" A whole new genus. Not merely a cross between this-and-that. But just like fish is a species, and man is a species—we are a new species. We can never fit into the general mold again. If you are an MIA (backslider) trying to fit in with the world, forget it. It's like a kitty trying to eat Friskies with a knife and fork!

God loves you, dear one. He has watched you for years. Every time you sat in front of a porno screen, He was there. Whenever you cruised into that Club, He was there. As you downed that bottle of

Scotch, or snorted that measure of cocaine, He was there. He was there as you walked away from the encounter that, at first, was so promising and exciting, but left you dead and hollow inside. He was with you those nights you contemplated the horrors of suicide. His eye has never been far from you; His ear is ever-tuned for your cry. When the hurting cry out, The Lord does hear. He will not turn away anyone who cries out to Him.

God loves you with an everlasting love and longs to have you saved. He has poured into me, this unworthy vessel, that same kind of love and desire. It is, of course, on a much smaller scale, because nobody can love you like Jesus can. Not your mother, father, spouse, friend, or lover—nobody can love you like He can, because God is love.

Here's the point: I am not out to "prove" that homosexuality is a sin, and has serious consequences.... I'm not here to jump onto your case and bawl you out, or hit you over the head with the consequences of your behavior. You know all that stuff. If you are reading these words, then God is calling you! Why can't it just be said that God's Word says it's a sin, and that settles it. We tend to complicate everything—why can't we keep it simple? I know about all the literature that twists God's Word to try to make homosexuality okay, but one fact never changes. Let's just settle it here in the beginning: homosexuality is fornication, and fornication is sin. Sin cannot get into heaven. Therefore, if we want to go to heaven, something has to be done about the sin. Homosexuality is fornication, because it is sexual behavior that takes place outside of marriage as prescribed by God in Genesis chapter 3. It is my personal belief that much of the fight for so-called marriage rights of homosexuals stems from this. Not only does it denigrate true marriage and the family, it can be another tool to justify the behavior. If homosexuals can have a "marriage," it is no longer fornication—thus, not a sin. Just something else for you to bite off and chew.

I am writing under the supposition that you, the homosexual, are secretly looking for a way out of your present lifestyle. You have tried it. You have lived it. You have seen it through—and have found it to be lacking. You have met with sorrow and shame, and wish with all your heart that there was a way out—a way back to God. You have discovered that it is not all that it's cut out to be. The only thing you have left that means anything at all is the feeling of belonging—the close community where others accept you. But you know that even this, too, will pass away. It's only a matter of time. You have been hurt. And you want out! But what about those desires? And how does it feel to come out? Nello...could you share something with us here?

NELLO: I found that coming out of homosexuality was really like being lifted up and out of a familiar world—out of "reality" as I completely believed it—and being dropped on a strange and scary new planet. That might be a slight exaggeration, but probably not by much. I also understand that the extremes of this will vary from individual to individual, depending on how deep they were into homosexuality—how much had already been damaged or destroyed.

The journey out begins with *you*, and it must be *your* choice. It must be in your heart, you must know for yourself that there's a big problem here ... you can't do it for someone else; you can't do it to get someone off of your back. The Lord knows your heart, and He will make the way. You don't have to understand it all, you don't have to have all the answers, you don't have to be "fixed" first.... nope, you just have to have a *desire* (and that does not have to be 100%, either, at first.) Your flesh will be fighting the war of your life.... But if you truly want out.... then it *will* happen. It can't just be when you get into a jam and decide to use the Lord to get you out. You need to reach a complete brokenness and cry out, "Lord, you are my only hope!"

LAD: That is true in every area of our lives, Nello. Paul knew it when he shared with us God's words to him: *"My grace is sufficient for thee: for my strength is made perfect in weakness."* And Paul's conclusion was that, when he was weak, then he was strong. Nello, there is something powerful, something truly awesome, in standing in our weakness before God. It is absolutely life-changing! (See I Corinthians 12:7-10)

My son, Joseph Stephen, was living for God in a powerful way. He was music director and involved in other areas of ministry. He could play any musical instrument and had never had a lesson. He had such a tender heart and really did love God. But he was hurt very deeply by his pastor. I'm not saying that to make excuses for him, because there is *never* an excuse to walk out on God. But it is a fact of life, and one that the church needs to address—what do we do with those who have been hurt to the point of spiritual death? We will discuss this more in Chapter Five.

Stephen was hurt over and over, but chose to stick it out. He had always been taught to obey the pastor. For one struggling with homosexual desires, and who has had no true father image, the pastor often serves that function. So when he wounds, it goes especially deep. Stephen still has not healed, and he needs to forgive.

Those of you who have been wounded by your pastor (shepherd), take heart. Read Ezekiel 34. When the shepherd drove them away, God did not beat them up. Instead, He says, *"Behold, I, even I, will both search my sheep, and seek them out... I will feed my flock, and I will cause them to lie down, saith the Lord GOD... I will seek that which was lost, and bring again that which was driven away, and will bind up that which was broken, and will strengthen that which was sick..."*

So take heart, MIA! God is not angry with you; He hurts for you. He has not turned away from you. He weeps for you. The way to mend His broken heart is for you to come home to Him. Run into His arms! Leave whoever it was who hurt you so badly—leave them in God's hands. Let God be the one to settle the score. Listen to me very carefully: The Word clearly says that if we do not forgive others, neither can God forgive us. (See Matthew 6:12, 14, 15; 18:35; Mark 11:25, 26; Luke 6:37; 11:4.)

So the question from my heart to your heart is: is it worth it, dear one? Is that awful bitterness you harbor inside so gratifying that you'd rather hang onto it and end up being lost for eternity? You have suffered enough because of that person—now it's time to let it go.

NELLO: As we step forward to come back to God—no matter what the history of our church experience has been—the Lord will open up a church for us ... He will place a pastor and a church family there for us that will have God's true love and compassion... yes, it's scary to take that first step. We fear that the same things will happen to us again.... but in God's time, according to His plan, and according to our heart, He will pave the way for us. We must be willing to follow that path.

LAD: I trust God. And I believe He will do that for Stephen. I believe with my whole heart that Stephen will return to the Lord and be saved. The hard part—as always—is the waiting for it to happen. Sometimes I will see unmistakable signs of his imminent return, and I'll get so excited and dance around my house praising God. Then, he is back to making the same old dumb decisions again—back to his sinning. This has to be one of the most frustrating walks possible.

NELLO: But don't you dare ever lose hope, Sister Doty! Stephen is coming back, and I have no doubt whatsoever about it. What I've seen happen is a series of small miracles... all along the way, day by day. It's a miracle that I'm telling you this stuff right now....

Here's the point.... we are in this for the long haul. At some point we've got to make the decision that this is it... *No matter what, no matter how long—period....* I'm going to keep on keeping on... that's what faith and trust are made of. No matter if we get knocked down, no matter what—once we make that commitment to never turn back—things will begin to happen. We must build a strong foundation in God's Word.... we must learn, study, be taught..... We pray for a heart that is teachable, we must know what is expected of us, what the Lord wants from us, how He wants us to live.....

And as we are doing this, we are also going to be building a new life for ourselves..... We leave all of our past behind. Now we begin making new friends, new activities, new relationships, new everything..... And that's not an easy task. It takes time for healing of all of our old distorted thinking, beliefs, and fears. We have to start learning how to relate to others in terms other than sex. We start learning what it means to be a male (or a female) as the Lord intended. There will be times of loneliness.... but as we continue, we will learn and find true and loving intimacy.... without sex. We will find belonging and inclusion with our church family... and we will find peace!

LAD: Will you tell us about how you found this peace, Nello? Will you give us your own testimony?

Nello's Testimony

"And they overcame him by the blood of the Lamb, and by the word of their testimony" (Revelation 12:11)

I can remember a time in the not too distant past that if anyone had told me I would be serving the Lord today and sharing with others about what He has done in my life, I would have laughed in their face. And if you had been a "Christian," I would have spit in your face. I hated the Church, I hated God, and most of all, I hated myself. But what a mighty and powerful and loving God we do serve! So here I am, serving the Lord, living a life that is according to His will, and giving Him the thanks and the praise for *everything* in my life.

As I look back over my life, I can recall as far back as the age of 4 that I "thought" I was "sexually" attracted to other males. Of course, at that young age I had no understanding of what the feelings I was experiencing were really all about. I had been a "mistake" from the moment that I was conceived. My parents did marry prior to my birth, but that marriage ended in divorce shortly after my birth. Not only did I not have a father in my life, but there were no other male figures in my life in the years to follow. All I knew was that I had this strong desire to be held, to be close, to another male.

In the years to come, the *real* reasons for those feelings would be twisted and distorted by the enemy. They would become the base for the subtle lie of homosexuality which was being laid in my young life. Eventually, I would buy them as the full truth. Event after event would be twisted, distorted, leading to yet another lie. Satan truly is the deceiver.

It was also at about the age of 4 that we began attending the local United Pentecostal Church. I don't think we ever missed a service. Sunday school was my favorite. We stopped attending church when I was around 11 or 12 years old. Throughout those early years a couple of things were going on in my life. First of all, that subtle lie was continuing to be built upon—that my attraction to males was in fact starting to turn to a sexual attraction, and second, God's Word and truth were being planted deep in my heart. And oh, how I thank God for that!

By the time I was 13 or 14 years old, I was able to understand that there was something very different about me, and I already knew that it was wrong. No one had to tell me that I had to hide my thoughts and feelings; I just knew it. I knew that the sexual attraction I was now experiencing toward other guys was wrong, and that if anyone ever found out, I would be in big trouble. This was the beginning of many years of guilt, shame and hiding what I was really becoming.

During high school I attempted the dating scene because that's what a guy was supposed to do, and I so much wanted to be like the other guys. I always double dated, and the only thing that was ever exciting to me on those dates was the fact that another guy was there. Even though I had "played around" with a few other guys while I was growing up, those experiences were always considered "a guy thing" even though I knew they meant a whole lot more to me. They were my first experiences of being able to find a form of closeness that I had longed for all of my life. The connection was made that sex was what provided the closeness, and would fill the emptiness and loneliness.

I had my first actual gay sexual experience when I was 18. At last, I knew that I had found what it was that I had been longing for all of my life—or at least that's what I thought! At the same time, the same old thoughts continued in my mind; I was bad, I was wrong. Of course, that's what I had heard from everyone.... gays are bad, gays should die, and God can't save gays! And the messages were not just about the sexual part of it; I kept hearing that everything about a gay person was bad. I ended up developing a sense of total worthlessness; a sense of not being fit to belong to anybody or anything.

After high school I joined the military service and actually had a great time for six years. Yeah, you guessed it; I didn't tell! And there were a whole lot of other guys that didn't tell either. So the sexual acting out continued and, equally as dreadful, it was also during this time that alcohol became my very best "buddy."

By the time I left the military, I was already a full blown alcoholic, but still able to function, and now, for the first time in my life, I actually looked into a mirror and called myself a homosexual. It was at that point that I accepted the label of "homosexual..." I had bought the lie. It was then that I dove headfirst into the gay community, and for the next several years pretty much lived in the gay bars and clubs, drinking, drugging, and sexually never being able to get enough. I loved every moment of it. This was *my* life. Sin was a total obsession. This was where I belonged and where I finally fit in and was accepted. For the first time. What an awesome feeling!

There was one short period when I did feel the Lord tugging at my heart, and I made a feeble attempt to live a life that was pleasing to Him. I was so under conviction as I made my way to the altar, repented, was baptized in Jesus Name, and was filled with the Holy Ghost. Because of all the old messages I had grown up with about how bad gay people were, because of fear of rejection, and because of my own shame, I was never able to discuss my struggle with homosexuality with anyone. I carried that secret and that battle alone, and this is the worst thing we can do. But the messages coming from the church at that time were not ones that encouraged me to reach out for help and support.

17

That is not an excuse for my life of sin; it's just a fact. But oh, the anger, bitterness, and resentments that I held toward God and the church. I soon returned to a life of homosexuality and did eventually hit bottom with the alcoholism, sleeping in hallways, and eating out of trash cans. Suicide became the only way out that I could see. But I had a mother who had never given up, who had never stopped praying for her lost son; and the Lord heard her prayers. I can still hear the door locking behind me as I was escorted into a state hospital for detoxification.

I was in a very restricted, long-term treatment program for almost two years, and I guess I am one of the few that never experienced a relapse after completing treatment. I was able to return to college, completed my undergraduate degree, and then was able to continue on to Graduate School. It was in Graduate School that I met the "love" of my life. To me he was the perfect guy; he was the one that I had always dreamed of. We were together for the next 10 years.

Then my world turned completely upside down. My partner decided that I was no longer the person that he wanted to spend the rest of his life with, and he moved on. At that time, I am not sure how I emotionally survived the breakup. He had been my world, pretty much my everything. Again, I am now able to realize that the Lord had always been there with me, that He had never forsaken me, and that He was now getting ready to offer me a way of escape.

Now the one thing that I never did discuss with my partner was my deep feelings and beliefs around being gay. When it came to spirituality and the life that I lived, I had been able to avoid, hide, run from, repress, deny, block; you name it, I did it. Or so I thought!

It took me a good year or so to heal to the point of being able to date again, and I was really starting to look for a new partner. However, there was one problem standing in the way—those words of God which I had heard in church as a little boy were still there, planted deep in my heart, and God had not yet given up on me.

As I am now looking back on my life, I realize just what a miracle it has been. There is no reason that I should still be here, still be alive. I will not discuss the details of the depth of the pit and of the perverseness that I had experienced and been involved in. I now realize that God was always there, and whatever His purpose was for me, He had spared my life. But the biggest miracle was just about to happen.

As I was starting to date again, I was perhaps further from God than I had ever been in my life. I really believe that my mind and my thinking were about 99.9% controlled by the powers of sin, my flesh, and the enemy. But, I still had that one, small, weak desire in my heart for God. And all God needs is .0000001% of desire for Him to take over and win the battle! During all of those years in homosexuality, I was so bound that I could not pray. Every year or so I would have an experience where I would mumble "God, please help me," "God, please get me out of this..." And that is no exaggeration. That's the very best that I was able to do. But that's all the Lord needed.

In early January of 1999, I was standing in my kitchen one morning, doing my usual morning putting around, having coffee, when I literally stopped, stood still, and cried out in a loud voice, "WHAT ARE YOU DOING?" I completely know and believe that at that moment God gave me back my mind and my ability to make one last choice. I realized at that point that I was going to go one way or the other.... period! If I entered into another relationship with a guy, that would be it, I would never reach out to God again. Or, it was time for God.

I immediately went to my computer and started searching for a UPC church. I knew there were none close by, but was hoping I might at least find one in the same State. The only one I was able to find was on the other side of the State, so I found a directory of names and email addresses for UPC members. And guess what I found?

Yep, I found a name..... And not only was this person very near to where I lived, but there was also a new home mission UPC church there as well. I was in awe, total awe. I had no idea. So I got real bold and sent off my email, asking about service times and requesting that I be added to their prayers. I received a reply back that same day, very friendly letter it was, asking if I might be able and willing to be a little more specific as to my prayer needs. Well, what did I have to lose? So again, I got real bold and typed the word "gay" in my next email. The email which I received back was the most loving, caring, non-condemning message that I had ever received in my life. It was also the most hopeful message I had ever heard about God's love for me and that through Jesus I could live a life that would be pleasing and in God's will. It also made it clear that sin is sin and that I was no worse because I happened to be gay. (God Bless you, Shawn!)

Soon afterwards I started attending church and was refilled with the Holy Ghost. Thank You Jesus! I was able to begin seeing myself in a whole new light. All of the old shame and guilt about being gay was lifted from my shoulders. No longer was I running, hiding, keeping that horrible secret all locked up inside. I was able to talk with my Pastor and with others in my church and receive their love, support, and prayers. What a total difference this had made!

The Lord has been so good to me since finding my way back to Him. Now don't get me wrong, I still have my days, still have my battles and temptations. But then who doesn't? The difference today is that I'm no longer alone, and God is now doing my fighting. He is giving me the strength and the desire to resist; He gives me the way of escape. As I continue to focus on building a real and a closer relationship with God, He continues to open my eyes and my understanding to my past. The old lies are exposed, replaced with the truth. I now realize that the little boy who was wanting to be close to another male was only wanting his daddy. I was experiencing natural feelings, natural needs, but the enemy twisted something beautiful and made it dirty. And day by day, event by event, the feelings and needs are being exposed for the lies that they were, and they are being replaced with God's truth.

Today I am truly able to say, *"Therefore if any man be in Christ, he is a new creature: old things are passed away; behold, all things are become new."*

3
Satan's Public Relations Department

Satan has much literature on the market that contradicts the Word of God. There are many writers who sound so pious, so spiritual and so knowledgeable. They know just how to distort the scriptures. They can take a verse and twist it so out of context that its readers say, "Wow! That makes sense!" Satan uses them to deceive the homosexual. Most Christians, when first entering the homosexual life, search for something from Scripture to say that what they are doing is not wrong. They don't want to turn their backs on God, so they seek something that will let them live the way they think they must, but with God's approval. And of course, Satan is right there, standing ready to provide. At just the right moment, some "friend" will happen by with all the "biblical" answers.

Satan is out to destroy marriage and the family, and to discredit our God any way He can. He wants to destroy people, because God loves us so much. He wants to cause all kinds of confusion and sorrow. Then there will be more people to point their finger at God and say, "Ha! What kind of God would let *this* happen?" Never mind that Satan is the one behind all the dysfunction in the first place. He is so jealous of God! He wants to destroy our love and trust and respect for a holy and loving God. What an effective way, by instigating the whole issue of same-sex relationships! Oh, Satan is sly! He's gradually gained control over the mainstream of America—education, television, radio, newspapers, publishers, and even the family-revered Disney.

You might be shocked by how much literature is on the market, written by so-called Bible scholars. These books are crawling with Satan's lies, twisting precious verses to say what he wants it to say...what he wants the confused to believe...his deadly snares. Listen to this, and I quote (Italics, mine): "Top scholars—such as Yale history professor...and New Testament professors... of Berkeley and...of Union Theological Seminary—show that those who perceive Bible passages as condemning homosexuality are being *misled by faulty translation and poor interpretation.*" (Helminiak, 1994)

This is from a book my son had on his coffee table during one of my visits. Imagine how I felt reading these lies from hell itself, and knowing my son had also read them. From the Foreword of

Helminiak's book, I read this: "There is no book I love more...than the Bible. Yet, had I not escaped the literalism of my Christian upbringing, I could not make that statement, for long before now I would have either dismissed the Bible as a hopelessly ignorant and prejudiced ancient religious document or I would have denied reality and become myself a small-minded religious bigot, using literal scriptures to justify my prejudices. A literal Bible, in my opinion, admits no other options."

I knew that Stephen had once loved the Word of God so much that, as a child, he had bought his own Thompson-Chain—on layaway. I could only wonder as I sat there in the solitude of his home: what did he think about God now, and His Word? I prayed and wept for a few minutes, then picked up the book again, and read: "...This author goes beyond the literal words... to enter into the spirit of the bible... dares to set aside the culturally conditioned biblical words for the power of his Lord...who embraced the outcasts of his society..." No mention of the many warnings not to add or take away anything from the Bible! No mention that God and His Word cannot be separated.

Listen to this, "As a Roman Catholic—and more importantly, a thinking person—I do not presume the Bible provides the last word on sexual ethics. In my mind, the matter is more complicated than that." (Helminiak, Daniel, What the Bible Really Says About Homosexuality, San Francisco, 1994. Not recommended for a scriptural study.)

I couldn't read any more. I didn't have the heart. I've included it here just so you will be aware of some of what is available "out there" for our questioning young people. I know that what I've just presented is only a tip of the iceberg! Our people need good, solid, biblical training! We need to start talking about this, and giving them proper teaching on it. People struggling with homosexuality—of all ages—are curious about it, and will get information one way or the other. Let's stop hiding our heads in the sand, and help them get what they need from us to teach the truth.

One wife told me she was desperately seeking information to help her cope with her husband's confession. She took secretly to the Bible bookstores but, not really finding a whole lot, she sought out other bookstores. She discovered a good-sized store called "something, something Light." The store carried gay and lesbian materials exclusively. She thought she'd surely find what she needed here, because a lot of the material included "Bible" in the title. She purchased a few and hurried home to begin her education about what went wrong with her and her husband. But as she read, her heart broke. It all spoke against her Bible...her God...undermined her Christian faith...attempted to destroy all that she held dear. By calling her names like "small-minded religious bigot."

LAD: Nello, I remember when I was in high school (yes, I can remember that far back!)...there was a rumor that people who wore green on Thursday were homosexual (we did not have the word "gay" back then, gay meant something else entirely). The rumor went that that was how they recognized each other, by wearing that particular color on that particular day. Well, the way I found out about the rumor was that one Thursday, I happened to be wearing green...and you know the drill. What about things like that? How do rumors like that get started?

NELLO: These are some of the things that have just been passed down from one generation to the next. They have heard stories, jokes; they have heard about one gay person doing something and then generalize it to all gays. Events have been twisted, added to, made up, and then have become "truth." Certain actions, behaviors—such as wearing green on Thursdays—have been identified as things that only gays do. And of course, some people have actually had a negative experience with one gay person and then will generalize that to all gays.

You were talking about books earlier, Sister Doty. Let me say here why I personally don't like the books that spend several chapters talking about how bad gays are. It's not so much about whether or not the information is correct or incorrect, and it's not about wanting to hide facts. And it's certainly not about wanting to paint homosexuality as being OK when it is just plain sin. But what that kind of book does is add to the already negative, hopeless image of who the gay person is. It reinforces within church members their unfounded fears of reaching out to gays. It also reinforces within the gay person that there is no hope for him and that the church does not want him.

My point is, why do we set out to "prove" that homosexuality is a sin? Why can't we say that the Word of the Lord says it's a sin, and that's that? If the Lord is not drawing that person, then we can talk till we are blue in the face and nothing will happen. But if the Lord has opened the door, then all we have to do is reach out with God's genuine love and compassion, and they will freely be led to the altar, to receive forgiveness and God's salvation. Let God do the cleaning up.... He does a much better job than any of us will ever do.

Many people base their opinions and understanding on what gay is, on what they see in the media. But what you see there is the sensational stuff—gay activists—that's what sells news, that's what makes it to the 7:00 news.

LAD: But gays do have a marketing plan, Nello, and this was revealed in 1987: "The first order of business is *desensitization* of the American public concerning gays and gay rights...You can forget about trying to persuade the masses that homosexuality is a *good* thing. But if you can get them to think that it is just *another* thing with a shrug of their shoulder, then your battle for legal and social rights is virtually won." (Kirk and Madsen, *After The Ball: How America will conquer its fear and hatred of Gays in the 90's*, p.47)

There is a real agenda, being promoted by the media—and where do they get this stuff they film for the news?

NELLO: There is always something happening when you go to places such as San Francisco and other areas where there is a large gay population ... and in such areas, you will find that gays have less fear of harm and, as a result, will come out and be more open. But what I'm saying here, Sister Doty, is that every single person has sat next to a gay person... you have done business with a gay person...you have gay family members...you have friends who are gay...and you don't have a clue that they are gay.

LAD: I can relate first hand to the ways the media have conditioned us. Right after Stephen first told me, there was this big parade and demonstration in the next town over. My immediate assumption was that he would be part of that—out there banging on the drums with them. After all that was "how gays are." But he was not a part of it and has never had an interest in getting out and demonstrating and displaying himself in public.

But at that point in my life, I knew very little about this kind of thing, only what I read in the media. And all I read horrified me. Most decent people *do* feel a horror and a sense of betrayal when hearing of these aggressive acts by homosexual organizations such as LAMBDA. I have researched this issue carefully over the past few years and am now aware of the most unfortunate fact that—because of the biased, politically-correct media—all homosexuals are judged by these.

NELLO: Which brings me to the subject of "loose talk," telling jokes, making fun of gays—or anyone else for that matter—and the damage it can do to somebody standing there with you and you don't know they are struggling with this. This is one of the reasons that people who are struggling with homosexuality keep it a secret and are not able to reach out and ask for help. They just turn around and walk away. You gave some excellent examples of this in your book, HELP ME HEAL.

Some other pieces of misinformation deals with issues such as how gays walk, limp wrists, talking with a lisp, dressing in a certain manner.... Decorating and arranging flowers, and a whole host of other behaviors which people believe mean that a person is gay. Now some of these may very well be more prevalent with gays, but it's not *because* they are gay. I remember one of my friends as a young person. He had this high pitched voice. I felt so bad for him, he was straight as an arrow, but he was made fun of and called names because of it.

For a bit of history here, in the early part of the 1900s, there were many sociological reasons that individuals who were gay, ended up "choosing" certain actions, behaviors, styles of dress, etc., and these ended up being labeled as a part of being gay.   Here's what I'm saying, the bottom line is that you can't always tell who is gay and who is not gay, just based on how they look, how they talk, how they dress, and what they like to eat. There is a very good chance that when you are talking with a friend and making fun of a gay person, that friend just might be gay.

"We Want Your Children"

LAD: A lot of people are frightened for their children to be around homosexuals. Do you have anything to say about that? What do you think? And what about the famous chant by the ACT-UP homosexual group in 1992: "We're here, we're queer, and we want your children"?

NELLO: Another very touchy issue is the belief that all gays are child molesters. This is just not true. There are gay people who have in fact molested a child, but heterosexuals also molest children. I would like to suggest that people, regardless of their sexual preferences, who molest children are pedophiles and that's a bird of a different color. Some gays have children of their own and they love them in the same way as anyone else. They love their nieces and nephews in the same way other people do. One of the saddest things that I have witnessed is the person who is gay, and out of fear that some action might be misjudged, have distanced themselves from their own family members. They stand back, and are afraid to hold their nieces and nephews.

LAD: I'm sorry to say that the whole Boy Scout issue is one that shows the hidden gay agenda. And there *is* an agenda, Nello—a political agenda—a *spiritual* agenda, headed up by the enemy of our souls.

NELLO: But this is not the majority. The point I am trying to get across here is that just because a person is gay does not mean that he is going to go around molesting children. Not all gays are like that. I was not!

LAD: Are you saying that there's never a time when we need to protect our children around them?

NELLO: I'm not saying that at all. I believe we should *always* protect our children. They deserve our utmost protection. And we need to train them, and instruct them in how to say "No" to anyone who tries to violate their bodies. We need to teach them to say No to anything that makes them feel uncomfortable.

LAD: The newspapers are full right now of case after case where priests have violated little boys. I think these cases are extremely tragic—but there are also cases where little seven-year-old girls are kidnapped from the sanctity of their beds, violated and murdered by male pedophiles. I also have personal knowledge of a priest who was giving instruction in first communion to a class of little girls. And all along, he was violating one of them. These are heterosexual, not homosexual, pedophiles.

NELLO: But we seem to focus on homosexuals... Nobody should be having sex, with anyone, outside of marriage. So it does not matter whether we are talking about homo or hetero, when any of us are outside the will and plan of the Lord, there is going to be a price that we will end up paying. Some teenagers think it's okay at their age. But experimenting with sex of any kind at this age can have a more profound influence and open doors that will lead them one way or the other. And, down the road, there will be a price to pay.

LAD: Yes, and part of that price is not only for the homosexual, but also his family and friends. If they could just realize the pain they will cause their spouses, their parents, and others who love them and care for their souls. I don't believe Stephen has a clue how many tears I have cried, how many floors I have walked. He knows it upsets me. He knows I can't approve of his sin. But he has no idea how deep the hurt goes.

The Spirit of Deception

NELLO: Homosexuals are deceived, Sister Doty—remember: their entire existence is built upon lies.

LAD: I've always said, the worst thing about being deceived is that we don't know that we are deceived. I would also venture to say that—of all groups of sinners—homosexuals are the most deeply steeped in deception. Satan has ordained this to be so. How else can human beings deviate so far from God's design—and bring so much destruction to their bodies and their minds—without being deceived into believing that it is not so.

God predicted this, He knew about it before the world began. And He warned us in His Word that there would be those who called truth lies, and lies truth, and other "Newspeak." Isaiah 5:20,21: *Woe unto them that call evil good, and good evil; that put darkness for light, and light for darkness; that put bitter for sweet, and sweet for bitter! Woe unto them that are wise in their own eyes, and prudent in their own sight!*

This is deception. There has been a spirit of deception unleashed on this earth as never before. And after it has done its damning work, God Himself will send a strong delusion. This great depth of deception is why homosexuality and other life-dominating sins are absolutely the hardest to break.

Deception abounds, of course, in the area of Bible interpretation. I do understand one thing, Nello, and that is that homosexuals are prepared with their arguments to refute what the Bible says. They are prepared for the newly-arriving Christian who is still full of doubts.

One of the most-often used arguments regarding the Bible is the scene between Lot, the Angels, and the men of the city of Sodom. When one reads this account through, there can be no doubt whatsoever that the Bible is talking about the sin of sodomy. We still use that word today; it has been handed down through all the generations. And yet, Satan has burned into the hearts of deceivers that this passage means just about anything else.

NELLO: Yes—it is most often described as the sin of lack of hospitality. Because hospitality is such an important topic in the Bible, some people can latch onto this explanation. But Lot told the men not to do wickedly—wanting to be hospitable is not wicked. People have to be deceived not to see the truth of this account, and that is that God destroyed Sodom for the particular sin of sodomy—homosexuality. If it was lack of hospitality, Lot would not have offered his virgin daughters. Lot knew. God knew. And we'd better know, too.

LAD: People leaving God to go into homosexuality are people who usually have been taught that the Bible is true. In their hearts they are loathe to do something that the Bible forbids. So here they are wavering, and very confused. Powerful cognitive dissonance! A part of them wants to stay in the church and another part of them is ready to give up the fight. This is the point where we—the church—can play such a vital role for them. If we can meet them at that point—and expound the scriptures to them, reinforce God's Word to them—and at the same time be willing to answer their questions and let them just talk....we can make a difference for that soul! Because if, at that very fragile point, they meet a seasoned homosexual, he will be more than willing to explain his version of what the Bible says. And it will not be what the Bible is actually saying. This is why I feel it is so important what comes over the pulpit. This person needs to sense that he will be listened to, and worked with.

Romans, Chapter One

Romans, chapter one, is another example. Homosexuality is spelled out there so clearly and anyone not wavering can see it. There is no question. Can we take a minute to look at a few verses specifically?

"Because that, when they knew God, they glorified him not as God, neither were thankful; but became vain in their imaginations, and their foolish heart was darkened." Romans 1:21-32

We can see the importance, Nello, of keeping our thoughts pure and clean. Paul tells us to cast down [hurl, throw] imaginations. If we allow and entertain these imaginations—("I wonder what it would be like?)—our hearts will become dark and ugly. Sin begins in the heart every time. When we entertain these thoughts, it will bring darkness to our souls.

"Professing themselves to be wise, they became fools."

Nello, I have known people who say, and actually believe, that they know better than the Word of God. They believe their way is better and that the Bible doesn't actually mean what it says. But you see, these people don't get to that place overnight. There are problems deep inside their hearts. For the homosexual, we have discussed some of those problems and then, when they reach the place of beginning to imagine what a homosexual relationship might be like, they have pretty much lost the battle.

That's why—if we can reach them at that point—those precious people on our pews—so many of them so young—we have a chance of saving them from untold anguish in their futures. These people who think they know best what is best are very foolish. Only a fool would challenge God in that way, and yet they think they are so wise. It's scary!

"Wherefore God also gave them up to uncleanness through the lusts of their own hearts, to dishonour their own bodies between themselves..."

It is so clear. The Bible talks about "lust" and about "bodies." People who try to argue these scriptures—hey, give me a break!

"...Who changed the truth of God into a lie..."

This is exactly what they are doing when they make the Bible say what they want it to say. This is what we have been talking about.

"...and worshipped and served the creature more than the Creator..."

This is the point where SELF has become their god. What feels good, do it. Don't deny myself any pleasure. "I deserve it." This will be reinforced for them over and over by their new "so-called" friends. "Ah come on, you deserve to enjoy life! You were in bondage so long!" It is a downhill journey from then on, more and more into selfishness.

"For this cause God gave them up unto vile affections: for even their women did change the natural use into that which is against

29

nature: And likewise also the men, leaving the natural use of the woman, burned in their lust one toward another; men with men working that which is unseemly..."

This verse is one that seasoned homosexuals like to quote. They take the word "natural," which is used twice here, and interpret it this way: they say that, if a homosexual would have intimate relations with a person of the opposite sex—that it would not be "natural." But Webster defines natural as, normal, accepted, expected. This is twisting what God has said. In the same sentence, the Bible declares that same-sex relations are "unseemly." Webster defines unseemly: Inappropriate, uncouth, improper, and unsuitable.

"And even as they did not like to retain God in their knowledge, God gave them over to a reprobate mind, to do those things which are not convenient..."

Again, when I look to Webster, "convenient" is defined as "suitable, fitting." And we can see something very important and very scary here: After the person has rejected God, God then rejects him. It took a long time for this to happen, but finally God gave them over as reprobates. Their future now is very, very ugly. Listen to the rest of this chapter:

"Being filled with all unrighteousness, fornication, wickedness, covetousness, maliciousness; full of envy, murder, debate, deceit, malignity; whisperers, Backbiters, haters of God, despiteful, proud, boasters, inventors of evil things, disobedient to parents, Without understanding, covenantbreakers, without natural affection, implacable, unmerciful: Who knowing the judgment of God, that they which commit such things are worthy of death, not only do the same, but have pleasure in them that do them."

So, Are You a Reprobate?

Nello, I'm sure you will agree with me that some people reading this will already feel they are perhaps reprobate. It's like the unforgivable sin that the Bible talks about. I've heard many, many people voice the fear that they had committed this particular sin. I even went through a period when I felt that I had committed it. I guess we all do at one time or another. Talk about depression and discouragement! I felt absolutely despondent at that point, to think I had committed a sin that God could not forgive.

30

But one thing I learned from that, which has been reinforced over the years since then—people who are afraid they have committed this sin, have not. And I believe that people who are afraid they may be reprobate, are not. In both of these groups—if they met the criteria for these things, they would not even be concerned about it. The fact that they are concerned shows me they have NOT committed the unpardonable sin, and they are NOT reprobates.

So what I say to you now, MIA, come home! God loves you! He has not given up on you! Your Father is standing at the door! The very fact that you are reading this proves it! If you were beyond hope, you would not care. You have not yet gone too far. You have not yet crossed that invisible line or you would not be reading these words. There is hope for you! God is waiting for you! Run, right now, into His arms!

4

Understanding Homosexuality

One of Satan's most dangerous lies you'll ever have to deal with is that the homosexual is "born that way, it's in his genes." The purpose of this lie is to instill hopelessness! But I am here to tell you that if you are gay, it is NOT in your genes! And if I were to tell you that it is, I would be telling you that you are a hopeless case. If you were born that way, and it is part of your biology, change would be impossible. For example, I was born with brown eyes. Today, over sixty years later I still have brown eyes. There were many times in my youth when I yearned to be a blue-eyed cutie, but the mirror always failed me. When I was born, my genes said I would be five-foot-seven, and sure enough—it happened just that way, even though there were times I felt awfully tall and gangly!

This "born-gay" lie has been repeated so many times that it appears to be scientific. It appears to be reasonable. If you are looking for an excuse to continue in your sin, it is an easy lie to believe. You don't feel so guilty. And if you help spread the lie, others won't think you're so guilty, either.

But if you are looking for an *escape* from this behavior, it is good news to learn that homosexuality is sin, not genetic. Because that means you can change, you are not stuck in this mode! We are stuck with our genes—but not with our sins. Hallelujah!

It's so simple; please try to see it. Repent, turn and walk away from it. Go the other way. I did not say it is *easy*. Nothing good is ever really easy. I said it is simple. Only Satan and his public relations department have complicated it and muddied the waters. There is great hope to be found in a gracious God.

Born that Way? Or God's Call?

But, for the sake of argument, just say—even if that were true—even if you *were* "born that way"—you need to remember this: celibacy is a gift. For His own reasons, God calls some people to celibacy. I believe this is a very special, precious call, because even our Lord Jesus chose that life for Himself while on earth. We each have a different call and a different path to walk with God. We have some awesome men and women of God today who are single, and are doing a tremendous work for the Lord. I know women evangelists who would enjoy it so much if the Lord sent them a husband—but since He has not, they have devoted their lives and service to the Kingdom of God. Look at the apostle Paul. *"But I would that all men were even as I myself. But every man hath his proper gift of God, one after this manner, and another after that"* (I Corinthians 7:7).

Have you ever considered that perhaps God is calling you or your loved one—not into homosexuality—but to a deeper kind of consecration, set apart unto Him? But that call could be interpreted, on a subconscious level, as an aversion to the opposite sex, thus homosexuality? Does what I'm saying make sense?

Satan says otherwise: he would try to convince you that you just can't help it; it is all beyond you, and that you're so weak and frail you simply must indulge in this lifestyle. But stop and think about it: I could be writing these same words to the college co-ed seeking an opposite-sex mate, because you see, it makes no difference—we *can* live a pure and celibate life—with God's help. I lived that way for almost 20 years. Paul tells us, *"...he that is unmarried careth for the things that belong to the Lord, how he may please the Lord"* (I Corinthians 7:32). The point is, no one has to have a sexual life! Heterosexual or homosexual. Sex is a gift to a man and woman who have been joined in holy matrimony. Any other use of it—homosexual or heterosexual—is sin, and is not the will of God. Sex is a powerful drive, but not one that has to be served at all costs.

NELLO: I know and believe that sin is sin, and that no sin is too big for the Lord to handle. I know that He will forgive all sins. But I believe that some sins—especially sexual sins, which are against our bodies—are more destructive; and as a result, the path out of those sins can be more difficult than for other types of sins.

LAD: I understand. Ungodly fear is a sin and will keep us out of heaven. Revelation 21:8 lets us know that the fearful are in the lake of fire right along with the unbelieving, and the abominable, and murderers, and whoremongers, and sorcerers, and idolaters, and all liars. And yet, I would not normally classify a panicky person along with a pornographer. We learn to think that we don't have sin in our lives because we don't commit the biggies—adultery, stealing, murder.

We begin to justify, and think we are righteous, when all along there is hidden sin in our hearts. We can be so overcome with unforgiveness and jealously, for example, that they develop into besetting sins. So whatever sin is in our lives, we had better deal with it because it's a life-and-death matter for our souls.

The Nature of Sin

I wrote about some of this in my book, MAXIMUM VICTORY (see order form on the last page of this book). Sin goes so much deeper than mere individual actions. Let me tell you why. Sin can become so entwined with our very nature that it actually becomes our disposition. Have you ever met a grump? No matter what you do, they are going to grumble, murmur and gripe. That is their nature, their disposition. That is how they are. They were not born that way. They became that way, based on past decisions to grumble, murmur and gripe. And then they say, Well, that's just how I am. You just have to accept me the way I am. Webster defines nature as: "The essential character of a thing; quality or qualities that make something what it is." He defines disposition: "One's customary frame of mind."

Applying this to the sin of homosexuality, we think of this as sin, but when it is done habitually, it eventually becomes part of a person's disposition. The sin of homosexuality becomes intertwined with a man's soul, like pouring ink into a glass of water—the water turns blue. That is why it is so hard to shake these kinds of sins—not because we were "born that way and can't help it"—but because it has become a part of "us." That, in addition to all the accumulated garbage—no wonder it's difficult to come out of this lifestyle.

NELLO: Some sins are more of a battle, and it can take longer to fulfill the scripture that "...the old passes away, all things become new." With homosexuality, my personal experience has been a *process* of the old passing away, and the new becoming, and replacing, what was the old man. And because of the damage that sexual sins, especially homosexuality, do to every single aspect of *who* we are, it might require "more" in terms of our focus and our dedication to the Lord. In other words, in coming out of these kinds of sins, we probably have to "jump in over our heads..." put all of our focus and energy on serving the God, drawing closer to Him, and building a stronger relationship with Him. Putting all our eggs in one basket.

LAD: Where does this leave deliverance?—taking away all ungodly desire for a particular thing—the Bible is full of it.

The Construction of Homosexuality

NELLO: God does deliver, no doubt about it. All sin stems from a lie from the enemy, but perhaps homosexuality is the biggest lie of all. It is one subtle lie after another, from our youth to the day that we finally accept the label for ourselves. Each one building on the other, with little "mistruths" added, with one word changed here and one word changed there.... And as we grow older, the events of the past become even more distorted, until the real truth about the event no longer exists in our minds. What we are seeing now is that past event through the eyes and memory of a lie. These are just built, one upon another, and we don't have a clue; we never realize what happened.

It can be compared to the construction of a building. You start with the foundation, then add brick upon brick. One thing on top of another until you have the finished product. And in the construction of a homosexual, that foundation, upon which everything else is built, is a lie. The whole package—the whole building—rests upon a lie! And the lies which follow hold it all together, like mortar.

LAD: This can be mind-boggling, it explains so much! Can you give me an example from your own life?

NELLO: Okay. I will. I remember one event when I was probably just about three years old. I was in church, and there was this guy, probably 16 or 17.... To me at that time, that was a grown adult..... I didn't have a clue to what I was thinking or feeling.... but I could not take my eyes off of him..... And every time I saw him, the same things were happening in my thoughts and feelings. Now this all got distorted in my mind as the years passed by. Then, as I was progressing into homosexuality and looking back on that event, I began to interpret it like this (distorted thinking): that, actually, I was truly gay at that time and that I was wanting to have sex with this guy. That was one of the most powerful lies Satan used against me, leading me to really believe that I had been born gay. When I came to the Lord, I totally, completely, honestly believed that I had been wanting gay sex when I was three years old! And, to my way of thinking, that proved that I had to have been born that way! It took a little time, and the Lord did destroy that lie. He opened my eyes to what really happened..... What was really going on all those years ago, was a little boy who didn't have a dad and was wanting his daddy, he was just wanting to be held and loved by a dad.... what I in truth was feeling and wanting was natural, healthy, and normal..... *I just wanted my dad!*

And so it's events like this that shaped future events, causing them to be distorted—something that they actually were not. One thing that makes all of this even more difficult to sort out, is that for each individual, events have a different effect...there is not one set "group of events" that will lead to the same outcome. The enemy uses whatever works on each individual. But the result is the same in the end.

I think with homosexuality, we become so alienated from everything that is normal and healthy, from what God intended for us.... we become so alienated from the heterosexual world, from family, from the church, from everything that we really need, and— yes, even alienated from God—from the sources that will help us, and we become more and more bound by the sin. We no longer are able to relate to the same sex in a Godly manner.... It's like we have burnt the bridges and have no place to turn but to our sin. And thus, we *become* the sin. "I *am* homosexual!"

LAD: You and the sin became one. It became your nature...your disposition. Your thoughts, and therefore your beliefs, shaped you into a pseudo-being—far removed from what your Maker created you to be!

NELLO: Any sin opens the door to other sins. And sexual sins just might open a bigger door..... When we sin, we cross God's line.... We take the risk and go against what is right.... There are things that keep us from sinning in the first place—different fears that sort of self-regulate us and so we honor those laws, whether of God or man. But when, for whatever reason, we rebel against them by sinning—that wall of protection is torn down...and so after we do that particular sin, and we don't get caught, that barrier between us and sin is decreased.... And so, with time, we will then sink deeper into more sin.

Telling a lie or committing homosexuality are both abominations to the Lord. But, will telling a lie put a "smaller hole" in

36

our protective shield than homosexuality? Or, is telling a lie just "more common," more accepted as not a big deal, and so we just mumble an "I'm sorry Lord," and go on our way. You see, these are all things we have to consider. So we ask, are all sins the same?

Life-Dominating Sins

LAD: Marlin Maddoux in his book, *Answers to the Gay Deception*, says:

> While it is true that sin is sin…it is also true that the Bible describes degrees of severity of sin. Jesus spoke of those who were more guilty than others, and who were thus liable for greater punishment (Luke 12:47-48). Romans 1 identifies idolatry and sexual sin as especially damaging, inviting God's judgment, and I Corinthians 6:15-20 singles out sexual sin. The truth is that in a sense, all sin is not the same. Murder and jaywalking are not equal in the total perspective of the Bible. In this light, homosexuality is shown to be a sin that requires firm exposure and action by those who are truly compassionate.

There is such a thing as "life-dominating sins." I believe homosexuality falls into this category. What that means is, the particular sin you are involved in controls your entire life. It bleeds into everything you do. The alcoholic's life is built around this drug. I know that's so, because I was an alcoholic. Everything I did was focused on the next drink. There are people who can have a glass of wine with dinner and it never bothers them. They can take it or leave it. But for me, one drink was poison. My life was dominated by alcohol. We read where Noah got drunk, but his life was not dominated by this sin. Other people's lives can be dominated by drugs… adultery… pornography…homosexuality. David committed an act of adultery, but his life was not dominated by this sin. He repented and turned away from it. The significance of life-dominating sins is that one cannot deal simply with the one sin; the entire life has to be treated. In the case of homosexuality, to try to treat the sin of homosexuality alone is a set-up for failure, because it affects everything they do. The homosexual must clean up his whole life. That is one of the reasons why, when the homosexual wants to be free from his bondage, he must forsake it all—friends, usual recreation, hangouts, literature—all of it, because it is all so closely meshed.

You Can Tell By Looking at Them—Right?

LAD: One thing I think convinces people they are gay is their looks and mannerisms. I've spent a fair amount of time around gay men. How do you explain that "certain walk" so many of them have? A certain "softness" about their face? And yes, the voice also. I've seen it in too many of them for it not to be some kind of pattern.

NELLO: I think that there are certain "traits" that one can be born with or develop as a child, that has absolutely nothing to do with homosexuality, but when connected to other events in their life, can possibly be used in laying the lie of homosexuality in their life. For example, some children are more sensitive than others. Some might in fact have a softer voice, might have naturally soft facial features...some have a gift for art, or a gift for music, and as they enjoy these, and learn to do them, they can receive a lot of negative messages, like "boys don't do that", or get called a sissy. Very often they are forced to *not* do those things and forced to do the "right things." Let's say a kid likes music and starts playing the violin..... Rather than wanting to go out and play baseball with the other boys, he wants to practice his music—it's something he loves! But now he gets called names, even his dad might be disappointed in him and call him names, might make him play ball whether he wants to or not .... Anyway, so the kid still likes the music.... but with all of the name calling, he starts thinking and feeling that there is something wrong with him, that he is different. You see where I'm going with this? So one thing leads to another—all of which are lies—and eventually, through twisted turns of events, he ends up in homosexuality.

LAD: It would begin with The Lie, then, and next would come the question...the doubts. Followed by the feelings of inferiority and shame.

NELLO: Now this will not cause every kid to end up gay, it varies from person to person.... but I think this is one reason why we end up seeing so many gays who are in the arts, music, are more "sensitive." So it's not because homosexuals play music, paint pictures, and write beautiful poems..... But they bought into that lie and ended up accepting the label for themselves and identifying themselves as such. Does that make sense? And I think this has become more true as more and more gays "come out of the closet," and as they more or less give themselves over to it.

LAD: I would like to comment on sensitivity, Nello. I have wondered so many times why, when there's a family of six kids, say, who are exposed to the very same environment growing up....and yet only one becomes gay. This used to puzzle me greatly until I realized that it is a matter of the child's perception of his reality. I teach all the time that it is not the circumstance that causes a reaction—it's our interpretation, or perception, of that circumstance. I believe the same is true here. My brother and sister and I grew up with the same parents, but had totally different perceptions of those parents. Now I think that gay men can be born with a gift of sensitivity, but that is not what makes them gay. If God has called a child into the music ministry, for example, I believe He has equipped the child. I think part of that equipment is a certain sensitivity. They were born sensitive, but not gay. However, it was that sensitivity that caused in them a different perception of the same reality.

The Devil's Red Herring

NELLO: Is it possible that homosexuality is one of the most subtle tools, tricks, used by the enemy to steal even more heterosexual souls? Think about this and let's just round off some numbers here.... let's say that in the U.S. there are 300 million people, and let's just say that 10% of the population is gay.... So we would be talking 30 million souls.... now that leaves 270 million other souls...

LAD: Before you go any further, I'd like to comment on that particular statistic, for the record. While there's no way of really knowing just how many gays we do have in America, 30 million is 'way too high. That 10% statistic has been used so many times that it has come to be accepted as fact by most people, including the media. That particular statistic came from the famous "Kinsey Report" back in the 1940s. But Alfred Kinsey's study at the University of Indiana was badly flawed. A careful reading shows that not even Kinsey, with his poor methodology, supports the claim of 10% homosexuality. Too many studies since then report between 1% and 4% --max. But, for the sake of argument, I'll go along with 2%. That's 6 million souls....now, what did you have in mind?

NELLO: Only this....is Satan going to settle for a mere 6 million souls? You think that'll keep him happy—6 million gays, while the other 294 million souls go free.....? I really don't think so. Let's take a look at what has happened within our churches around the issues of fornication and adultery. Is it possible that homosexuality has become a "rallying point," an issue that everyone can join in on and say Amen to because it does not affect them—and so the focus is on "those homosexuals?" And in the process, the focus is taken off of fornication and adultery and divorce, and the destruction of our families. You mentioned in your book, HELP ME HEAL, about there almost being two sets of standards. But the bottom line is that sin is sin. I'm thinking just how complicated this issue is..... And it's sin that makes it complicated..... If we just did what God wanted us to do, there would be no such complications.

LAD: So what you're saying, then, is that homosexuality may well have become the scapegoat?

NELLO: I believe it could. It is possible that fornication and adultery are not only destroying the family, destroying homes, lives, but also opening the door for other sins. Is it possible that as the issue of homosexuality is being used by the enemy to take the focus off of fornication and adultery, that the enemy is stealing, killing, and destroying even *more* souls. And they are just slipping away and no one is even seeing what is happening, because we have our eyes on the "biggie"—homosexuality—while Satan is reeling in the souls.

LAD: I am glad you brought that up, Nello, because we are getting into something very important here. Homosexuality is just the tip of the devil's iceberg. One point I want to make is that it does not matter a whole lot the *Why*, or the psychological underpinnings of homosexuality. The best use that kind of information might be put to would be in the area of prevention. One thing that has come out of my training in psychology is that God's Word goes straight to the heart of the matter, whether we understand things or not. I remember as a psychiatric patient, I'd spend many, many hours trying to understand why this, or why that. And then finally! I'd understand! But nothing changed. Not really. Not until the Spirit of God came to live within my heart.

I once knew a man who was one of the world's biggest haters of gays. He would preach and teach and holler all the time, always drawing attention to it. He's the one I thought of as you were talking about the enemy's focus on this one aspect of sexual sin. Because all the time this man was coming against homosexuality so hard, he was seducing young ladies in the church. I'm not saying that he was consciously aware of what he was doing, but it is an example of how humans can be used by the enemy to get God's people off track.

There are so many faces of evil, and it has existed for so long. Evil is not something new. But the force of evil, and the power behind it, is growing increasingly stronger in these last days. Homosexuality is just a drop in the devil's bucket. A step on the way to more evil things. That is another reason why it is so important that we reach out and help save these souls from certain death. Save them, pulling them out of the fire (Jude 23)!

5

A Special Kind of Evil

My pastor, Nathaniel J. Wilson, recently preached a message at The Rock Church that I feel needs to be shared. He got into so much really deep stuff, that I cannot include a whole lot of it here, but parts of it are incorporated into this chapter. As I sat in that service, I began to see that the sin of homosexuality is merely the tip of the iceberg that Satan has diabolically planned for this earth and for God's children. I sat in that service thinking, why bother doing this book on homosexuality?—the problem is so much bigger!

I suppose what I am trying to say in my own humble way is that, if you are into homosexuality today, the path you are walking is far more dangerous than you ever imagined. The destination that awaits you at the end of that path is far more horrible than your darkest nightmares. I do not say that to frighten you or threaten you, but I believe we need to see the big picture—far beyond such things as absent fathers and child molestation and name-calling. We walk in a world that is unreal, but amid very real enemies that we cannot see.

My husband and I were getting a quick bite recently in a fast-food place in the front of a Wal-Mart. As he went to get the food, I sat watching a lady and her little son at the next table. She wore tons of makeup, things in her ears, tattoos all over her bared body, and she was committing an obvious sin in front of her son. In fact, I saw later, she had induced him to participate. I withdrew into my little shell, allowing a critical spirit to speak to me. The pattern Christians follow is like this: we shudder at what we see, and pull away from it. We think something like, "How can they!" and then become critical. Then we form a judgment about them. Then we condemn them. That was the path I was on that afternoon.

Suddenly the Lord broke into my thoughts and chastised me. He reminded me that this is *her* world, not mine. I am just passing through—hopefully on my way to heaven. I am not to mind the things of the world or let them get to me. He did not ask me to witness to her, or to rebuke her of her sin. He merely asked me to stop and take a look at myself. And repent of what I saw!

Isn't this how we typically respond when we see a homosexual? The point is that we do indeed live in a world that has nothing to do

42

with reality, but the choices we make daily happen to deal with the reality of heaven and hell. Hindsight is always clear, and it is easier to look back and see the progression of sin in a life, but while it is being lived, it is usually done in a state of blindness. A magazine centerfold leads to something else, and that leads to something else, and eventually pornography has consumed a person's every thought and action, and finally, his very being. Pornography no longer is enough to satisfy. The person must find an outlet for it—such as the Ted Bundy case. If a homosexual were to stop for a moment and look back to the time when he first made the decision "just to try it once...." He would begin to see clearly how the progression was actually set up by the enemy of his soul. This is why our focus is so important. It is vital that we keep our minds clear and clean and free of evil.

Bishop Wilson began his message with the scriptural passage from Jude 4-8. Take a moment to read this for yourself. Then he says, "Evil as never before is coming upon us. We need to be cognizant of it. This is not your usual kind of evil—it is something far more sinister, much deeper and darker than even the drug culture and sexual depravity. The primary difference is that this kind of evil also has a spiritual component that goes beyond what people do with their bodies. It goes into spiritual idolatry, such as in the Old Testament. These days we do not usually think of idolatry as all that serious—if we think of it at all. Idolatry is only the idols in the Bible—those little iron and brass gods that people would fall down and worship.

"Idolatry in the Old Testament," Bishop Wilson explained, "referred to spiritual fornication. That is from the Greek pornea, and included far more than adultery and fornication. It could be defined more as interaction of human beings in a morally depraved state with the spirit world, in an area that goes beyond what normally can be classified or categorized.

"Spiritual depravity always leads to spiritual destruction and to ultimate abuse and destruction, as well as physical, emotional, mental and intellectual total breakdown."

Satan's Ultimate Goal

"Satan's ultimate goal is to seduce people into this kind of destruction. 'Normal' evil is not enough for him. In every ancient heathen religion—from ancient Rome, Medes, Persian, Babylon—idolatry always intermingled with sexual immorality—take, for example, the

43

temple prostitute. And when idolatry enters into the arena of worship, it goes far beyond the garden variety of depravity. It goes into an area where the spirit of man is caught up in it and there are spirits in places that specialize in this. Jude 13 lets us know that the kind of evil we are now describing does not derive from any natural sources. It is a power so strong, it overrules people."

Homosexuals may or may not be possessed by evil spirits. If they have totally and absolutely given themselves over to this sin—it is possible that they have sunk into an area where they are being controlled by demonic spirits. They become as enslaved to their sexual drives as Hitler was to eradicating the Jews.

Jude 6 says that the evil angels left their habitation; the result was that they were caught between two worlds—caught between what they were, and what they wanted to be. In other words, they were caught between being a heavenly species and an earthly species. This is like the MIA when he walks away from God. Having been born again as a new species, he will never fit in the earthly realm.

In I Corinthians 11:10, we learn that women have power on their head, and they should keep their hair uncut, because of the angels—the early church fathers connected it with what we are teaching in this chapter—that the cutting of her hair is a sign of rebellion in a woman, and she opens herself to the same spirits of these Genesis sons of God—and they still exist today! A submissive woman's hair is her protection. The demons (angels) see this and must respect it.

"We are going to see more people caught in the web of ungodliness, and there will be a domino effect. Watch out for bitter people. And keep a watch for any root of bitterness in your own soul. Bitterness is a key component of spiritual depravity! These spirits are predators, stalkers, blood drinkers; they will bring you down and then laugh about it with glee. It's a powerful spirit that sweeps you into it."

Brother Wilson said, "Throw your television out. Get the filth and depravity out of your home. There are educators who do not even know Jesus Christ who will tell you the same thing." The man who invented the television said the same thing, near the end of his life. You cannot feed on garbage without getting sick. Once I was counselor on a church staff, and I ran into a mystery. I would counsel people all week long, and when they left the counseling session, there was already much improvement because they had begun to understand how to apply God's Word to their lives. Then they would return the next week, just as bad off—sometimes worse—and this happened over and over. I could not understand it, until the Lord revealed that they were leaving His Word and His counsel, and going home to feed on soap operas and racy dramas! No wonder they were so discontented! What ordinary Christian woman can stand up under the glare of the glamour queen of television?

The same can be said about romance novels. I speak out against them every chance I get. Throw them out of your house! Stop feeding on the unreality. No Christian husband can compare to the wild and sexy, rich and handsome, young protagonist of these books! They will break up your marriage, ladies. They will lead you astray.

Hollywood, the whole movie industry—study the lives of these people. Bishop Wilson says, "I am not trying to hurt them because we love them. If they were in this church, we would love them and help them and work with them. We long to see their souls saved. But they are caught in the lies! They are caught in sinister, viciously evil destruction. They are powerful spirits that have hold of these people."

Many of you are too young to remember the innocence of the forties and the fifties. As a young girl, I can remember meeting a friend half way between my home and hers, and walking her back to that point late in the evening. We were not afraid. If I ever experienced fear while walking alone in the dark, it was fear of monsters or some such thing left over from a Frankenstein movie—we never thought about rapists and murderers and tormenters stalking us. It was a safe and innocent era.

Along came television. At first the stories were innocent—screen married couples even had twin beds in those days. But it has been a downhill progression. The removal of prayer from the schools. Legalization of abortion. Indecency has gradually infiltrated our senses. What was once inconceivable is now among the usual. It is a downward spiral. It is a slippery slope; once it starts sliding downward, there is no stopping it.

Today young children in supermarket lines are exposed to hardcore pornography. I tell my grandsons, you *must* look straight ahead, you *must* guard your eyes! And I will not even begin to elaborate on the evils that the Internet brings into our homes. What once were difficult and embarrassing methods of obtaining pornography has become comfortable, in the privacy of our own homes via computers.

Sin always escalates if it is not repented of. We sink deeper and deeper into it. And that is why homosexuality is only the tip of the iceberg. While we become so fixated on one particular sin, all around

45

us it is growing darker, and we fail to sense it. Satan has no intention of stopping with homosexuality. It is only his beginning. For many small tots, he lays the trap. Take away the daddy. Make the mama tough and independent in order to survive. Confuse the child as to who and what he is, and where he belongs. Inject him with strange feelings, bizarre thinking. Isolate him at school and home. Fill his imagination with things unthinkable. You see, Satan knows the Bible—he knows Proverbs 22:6: *Train up a child in the way he should go: and when he is old, he will not depart from it.* He will snatch them as young as he can! With any lie he can!

It used to be that the majority of homosexuals led quiet and peaceable lives, blending in with the world around them. But growing numbers of them have taken the bait of the enemy, and followed him into the depths of depravity. Ronald Fung comments: The sin of "indecency" may represent and advance on "fornication: [immorality]; and "impurity," for it is vice paraded with blatant impudence and insolence, without regard for self respect, for the rights and feelings of others, or for public decency. Here is precisely why indecency is such a terrible thing. It is the act of a character which has lost that which ought to be its greatest defense—its self respect and its sense of shame. (Fung, The Epistle to the Galatians, p. 255)

The Power of Purity

Brother Wilson goes on: "A pure heart is a strong heart. Believe God. Whatever you say, Lord, that's the right thing for me to do. Out of that kind of heart develops the Power of Purity, as opposed to the Power of Evil. Every leader is commissioned by God and is given authority in their area as a child of God. When the Power of Purity meets the power of evil, the Power of Purity could stare it down and say *You're Guilty!* Your home needs this power. Your life needs this power."

Do you see how Satan has purposed in his evil heart to destroy it all by stealing our purity! Adam was given power over the beasts of the earth and the fowls of the air. When you read the Bible, fowls are indicative of evil spirits. God was telling Adam, I give you power over the prince of the air. This is what it means to know Jesus who came to set the captive free, to open the prison doors, and liberate people from their sins.

"The source of their evil-ness is not conceived in their own imagination but is from deep in the subterranean intestines of the earth and spirit world. Belching out of there. A place where the worm dieth not and the fire is not quenched. There are preachers out there laughing about separation from the world. If you know one of these, you'd better distance yourself from them, for they are going toward becoming reprobate themselves.

"What all of this amounts to is a contest between following the word of God and falling into—through ignorance or willfulness, either one—the clutches of a depravity that is indescribably evil. We need to go to God and repent unto God. Deliver us from evil! For if ye forgive men their trespasses your heavenly father will forgive you, but if you forgive not, your father will not forgive....It is time now to lay it all on the altar. All those temptations, the ill will, the bitterness, the anger...it's time to lay it all on the altar. That one who hurt you and abused you, the one who lied to you and stabbed you in the back...it's time to forgive."

Parts of the above were quoted from a message by Nathaniel J. Wilson at Sacramento, CA, January 6, 2002

Rebellion and Witchcraft

For rebellion is as the sin of witchcraft, and stubbornness is as iniquity and idolatry. Because thou hast rejected the word of the LORD, he hath also rejected thee from being king.
I Samuel 5:23

Saul was hand-chosen by the Lord to be Israel's first king. He was a humble man, small in his own eyes, and he loved God. But that all changed. He became the kind of man who thought he knew best, and that his ways were best. And as much as God loved Saul, He had to reject him from being king. God never rejects us first. We are the ones who reject God. And He will follow us--loving us, wooing us, trying His best to draw us back to His arms. But we are stubborn! Idolatrous! Rebellious! And rebellion is as witchcraft.

Witchcraft is not a harmless game, and a witch is not an old lady dressed up in a costume with a pointed hat. Deborah Randall, author of *Treasures of Darkness* and other warfare books, battles witchcraft constantly. She defines it, "Witchcraft is the base spirit from which all evil spirits are derived. Lucifer was preeminent and jealous of God and desirous of power. His rebellion cost him his position in heaven. Once banished, he had to find a way to fight God and His church while fueling his desire for power and preeminence. This he accomplishes through witchcraft. Witchcraft is the adversary's religion and its purpose is to hunt down and destroy the soul of man. Those who are dedicated to this evil cause actually go on soul hunts. Anything that is anti-God has been belched out by this spirit. Destruction is its main objective and woe to the souls that are caught in its clenching jaws."

The rebellion of the angels following Lucifer echoed throughout all of heaven. This rebellion ended with one-third of all the angels leaving God. Rebellion is a serious and grave sin. Rebellion is as the sin of witchcraft. And homosexuals live in a state of rebellion. Oh no, Sister Doty, I am not the rebellious type—I'm for peace, and getting along with everybody. I am a very gentle sort.

No, you are rebellious. You are rebelling against everything God ordained for you. You are rebelling against God's perfect plan for you in the very first chapter of Genesis. Look at 1:27: So God created man in his own image, in the image of God created he him; male and female created he them.

Have you ever wondered why God took Eve out of Adam's side? Why did He not gather another dust ball to make Eve? This verse explains it. Eve was created at the same time as Adam. She already resided within Adam. She was already a part of God's image. Adam and Eve were one. And since woman already resided in man, all God had to do was "extract" her.

Verse 28: And God blessed them, and God said unto them, Be fruitful, and multiply, and replenish the earth.... Now the sacrament of marriage begins to be clear. It was instituted in Eden, and from these scriptures we see that marriage is the putting back together again of the male and female. This is why God says, that upon marriage, husband and wife become one. That is why a homosexual union is unnatural and transgresses the law of God.

God told Adam and Eve to be fruitful and multiply, and replenish the earth. It is impossible for those of the same sex to do that. They may adopt a child, but that is accommodating—it is not replenishing. It is not multiplying. It is not obeying God's command. In other words, it is rebellion.

Spiritual Abuse

Satan loves rebellion! If he can get God's people to rebel, he has made great strides in stealing that soul away from God. Most people who go off into rebellion never make it back. Unity and harmony in the church is vital. It means so much to God. Satan knows this, and will do all he can to stir up strife.

I travel to churches across the country, and everywhere I go I find saint-and-pastor feuds. It seems like some in the ministry are bludgeoning the saints to death. Too many pastors are not complying with God's blueprint for shepherding, and too many sheep are scattering, and dying, as a result.

What is a saint to do when his or her pastor acts as a "lord over God's heritage?" How should a saint respond when his pastor becomes a dictator, and the sheep are bleeding? There is far too much backsliding over this. There are too many MIAs hiding out from the ministry—which results in them hiding out from God.

Obey them that have the rule over you, and submit yourselves: for they watch for your souls, as they that must give account, that they may do it with joy, and not with grief: for that is unprofitable for you. (Heb 13:17)

The dilemma is that the Bible says we are to obey those that have the rule over us—even when we are dying? Sister Doty, the Bible says that they are supposed to watch for our souls. How can the Bible say they are doing that when they are killing us spiritually?

I heard a saint just yesterday roar: "I *refuse* to sit under a pastor who is a dictator!" He has been hurt by the ministry many times, and has allowed bitterness to grow. He sits under no pastor now, and I fear for this poor man's salvation. Anger and rebellion pour out of him. He went on to say that God would not require him to sit under a pastor who was not obeying the Word. Thus, our dilemma.....

I Peter 5 holds the key to the dilemma. Peter was a man who understood things like rebellion and impulsiveness. He was always getting into trouble. In this chapter, Peter is writing, first, to the elders, or pastors; and second, to the laymen.

49

The elders which are among you I exhort, who am also an elder, and a witness of the sufferings of Christ, and also a partaker of the glory that shall be revealed: Feed the flock of God which is among you, taking the oversight thereof, not by constraint, but willingly; not for filthy lucre, but of a ready mind; Neither as being lords over God's heritage, but being ensamples to the flock. And when the chief Shepherd shall appear, ye shall receive a crown of glory that fadeth not away.

--1 Peter 5:1-4

These verses, then, are the blueprint which pastors are directed to follow. God loved His church. God wanted His church to be fed, and He wanted the shepherds to feed with love, not out of duty or obligation. Do it with a willing and loving heart, because the sheep belong to Christ and He loves them!

Peter provides the blueprint, and then the reward for those who follow it. These injunctions are between God and the elders, not between God and the saints. It is the elder's responsibility to obey. If he does not, he will have to answer to God.

Next, Peter addresses the saints in verse 5: *Likewise, ye younger, submit yourselves unto the elder. Yea, all of you be subject one to another, and be clothed with humility: for God resisteth the proud, and giveth grace to the humble.* Verse 6: *Humble yourselves therefore under the mighty hand of God, that he may exalt you in due time:*

We see here the urgency of humility. If we go to one another with humble hearts, peace and harmony will reign. You cannot be angry with someone who is begging your forgiveness with tears streaming down his face!

On the other hand, God resists us when we are proud. He is not pleased and, depending on the depth of it, we can fall under His wrath. It is a fearsome, hurtful thing to be under submission to a prideful pastor. But, according to the Word of God, that is what we are called to do. And this is where the trouble starts. Some saints will buck up and refuse. They get these two parts of Peter 5 mixed up. They take seriously the first four verses and demand compliance by their pastors. If the pastor is not complying, they feel that releases them from their obligations, set forth in the remainder of that chapter. But that is not what the chapter says.

How, then, does one function under these circumstances? And how is it that one half of a church will be slain by a particular pastor, and not the other half? I believe that, if saints will respond the way Peter explains, they will emerge from their nightmare victorious and strong, instead of defeated and bitter.

We are to let God fight our battles. Verse 7 tells us to cast these cares upon Him, because He cares for us. And then, in the very next verse, verse 8, Peter tells us why we need to go through our nightmare with a sweet and humble spirit: *"Be sober, be vigilant; because your adversary the devil, as a roaring lion, walketh about, seeking whom he may devour."*

The enemy of our souls has set the whole thing up, do you see? If erring pastors can just realize that they are playing into the hand of the enemy, that the enemy is using them to destroy—I should think they would repent in sackcloth and ashes!

Peter goes on in the next verses—read them for yourself—to warn saints to resist this enemy, don't give in to him, don't play into his hands. Peter also lets us know that we will suffer under this pastor. Now that is the point where most saints will walk out. When the suffering gets bad, they leave and either become MIAs or move on to another church. But here is how Peter states it: *"But the God of all grace, who hath called us unto his eternal glory by Christ Jesus, after that ye have suffered a while, make you perfect, stablish, strengthen, settle you."*

So when we look again at Hebrews 13:17, *Obey them that have the rule over you, and submit yourselves*—we realize that the Word means exactly what it says. It does not give us legal loopholes through which we can squirm out of a painful situation. It tells us to ride it out. And it tells us how.

A Personal Experience

My children and I were once in such a church. It had started out so good, and ended up so bad. I began to die spiritually under the so-called leadership of this man. My son was dying, also, right before my eyes. The hurt penetrated my soul, and I saw no way out of the spiritual devastation, except to leave. I finally asked for a transfer. He denied it and threatened me if I left. I would be a doomed person if I walked out those doors.

I did leave, and the wake that followed was so destructive. I made several attempts to go back but they all failed. My two children remained there. My son, who had always been taught to obey the pastor, hung in there until he died a spiritual death. When he finally left, he was a walking dead man. My daughter survived.

As I look back on that time of horror, I wonder what I should have done differently. Hindsight is flawless. I know now that I should have stayed and seen it through. But I ran for my spiritual life. I did not know how to handle it, or how to lead my children through the minefield.

As I was thinking about this chapter, I began to ask God to help His people understand how to handle these types of things. What is it that makes the difference? Why does one person backslide? Another one run away? And another one survive? I went to God with this, and He told me that, when we submit to a pastor who is not living up to God's guidelines of caring for His church, we are not to submit as unto the *man*—but unto God.

Colossians 3 gives us wonderful instruction for all walks of life, and informs us that we are to do everything in the name of the Lord Jesus, while at the same time having a heart full of thanksgiving. If we try to submit to the *man*, we will slowly grow hard and brittle. Colossians 3:23, *And whatsoever ye do, do it heartily, as to the Lord, and not unto men.* And that, my friend, is the key. That is the way to survive when all around you everyone else may be dying. We are to submit heartily—with great gusto!—not sullenly and resentfully.

The next two verses spell out our reward, or our punishment. Then the conclusion of the matter is that there is no respect of persons. God does not show favorites. If the pastor is wrong, God will take care of it. God will deal with it according to His Economy. And if the saint is wrong, God will do likewise. You see, we do not have to worry about it. Our job is to submit heartily [jovially, energetically] to the Lord, and leave the elders in God's hands. The Word promises us that God will take care of everything. His word to you: "Relax, honey—everything's going to be all right!"

Our job as ministers is to guide and love and feed and help however we can. It is not to order around, boss, threaten, or to be lords over God's heritage.

I have gone into this detail here because so many who leave the church in anger and hurt because of an errant pastor, drift into homosexuality. The connection is the rebellion. Another father-figure has betrayed them.

Most homosexuals harbor deep bitterness and unforgiveness. Don't allow these things to grow inside of you, to become even the root of bitterness which defiles many. Get it out! Put yourself under the hand of a living and loving God. Don't allow this special kind of evil to begin to grow up in your heart. If it has already, God can take care even of that, if you will let Him, and if you desire it. You do not have to continue living in the graveyard of evil. You can make your own altar right there where you are today and lay it all down before God, crying out to Him, that you've tried it your way and it hasn't worked. You've gone your own way, done your own thing, searching—looking for peace and a scrap of happiness—and it just has not worked. But I am here to tell you that you can have it all. There is a price to pay, but you can have it all. You can have the peace of God that surpasses understanding. You can have joy flowing out of you.

6
Words to the Church

People make fun. They ridicule. I can't find a record where Jesus ever laughed at anybody. The lepers, the outcasts of His day...He only showed them love and healing. You see, you never know what might be going on in the heart of the one standing beside you. One youth, after he had left the church and drifted into the gay lifestyle, told me this story: He had been struggling for years with identity problems. His father had left him, and he longed for the strength and comfort of his father's love. In the midst of these struggles, he was seeking someone in the church he might be able to talk to, to help him sort out his feelings and get back on track.

Shame on the Field Trip

He finally decided he would take a chance with the youth pastor. It was during one of their outings. Some in the group were walking along a levee, when an obviously homosexual pair strolled by. My young friend stole a glance at the youth pastor and as he did, he saw the pastor jab the boy walking beside him and sneer. My friend's heart broke as he watched the two of them begin to laugh and make ugly remarks. He knew right then he would not be able to make himself vulnerable to this pastor. Broken and confused, he ended up drifting away, and is far from God today.

Oh people, be compassionate! The pastor did not intentionally hurt this youth. It was a thoughtless thing that turned out to be a devastating thing. The Bible has a lot to say about idle words. I'm not saying we can't talk about this subject, and agree together on what the Bible says about homosexuality. We should never water down the truth, and we have to speak against it. But we need to watch how we talk, because we never know who is watching us, and what repercussions our speech might have.

Shame in the Pulpits

Some of the things I've heard from our pulpits bring me shame. It is right that we preach against this sin. These days more than ever, we need to sound the trumpet and speak out against it. But there is a proper way to do that. I have had people criticize me for this stance. To answer that, I look to Jesus, who should be our model. Jesus, in His most furious moments, did not make fun and ridicule. He spoke out— strongly—using words like "vipers," and "hypocrites," "fools..." Listen to Jesus in Matthew 23:33 *"Ye serpents, ye generation of vipers, how can ye escape the damnation of hell?"* That is strong language. Read the passage for yourself in Matthew 23; start up a few verses, about verse 10. Hear that strong language. Jesus never minced words. And yet He never joked about a person's condition or made fun of their sin.

I've seen pastors display their "limp wrist" and swing it all around. I've heard them mimic the high-pitched voice. I once witnessed a pastor actually don high heeled shoes and prance around the platform. Inside, I felt like dying. What a spectacle he was—and how ignorant. Did he really believe that's what gays did? I happened to know someone in the congregation that day who wanted out of homosexuality. This man was not "effeminate." He didn't walk around with limp wrists and girlie sounds. He was looking for help, but realized he would not find it in this church, and he walked away, back into the world from which he had emerged.

It is easy to say, "Well, why don't they speak up? Why don't they just stand up and be strong? Fight! They need to fight!" It would be wonderful if they could just ignore the pain as their old wounds opened up afresh. In their beginning steps of their journey back, they are not strong yet. Their souls are being pulled, and torn apart, every which way. The enemy is whispering in their ear ninety-miles-an-hour. He is determined not to lose them! He will fight hard to keep Jesus from having them!

Please don't criticize me for being too "soft." I would rather err on the soft side any day, than judgmental. Again, when I look to Jesus as a model, I see Him weeping, and everywhere throughout the gospels, He looks upon the people with compassion. His touch is gentle and caring.

Shame in the Social Hall

There was a sister in the church whose son had just gone into the gay lifestyle. I knew what she was going through, and so did the pastor. She had decided not to allow anyone else in on her burden, to bear her pain alone. I watched one day at a social in the dining hall. She was bravely trying to hold up, carrying her secret pain. Then one of the ladies brought up the subject of homosexuality, and the other sisters joined in. Before long, there was laughing and joking and making fun, and I watched my friend's face fall. She was crushed. Oh, what pain and shame could be spared, if we would just watch our idle words!

I know first hand the hurt that these careless words can bring. People, not knowing about my son, have made jokes in front of me. I felt like crawling under the table. Once, a minister said something to the effect that homosexuals can never be saved. Homosexuality is *not* the unpardonable sin, but if that is truly your belief, then please don't voice it. You never know if some precious wife or mother or husband, desperately needing faith for their homosexual loved one, is standing nearby. Don't destroy what little faith they might have left. Now I suspect that, had these people known the pain I was in, they would have held their remarks. But that does not change the fact that they would say them in other places, and in front of other people—maybe others who might be hurting as I was.

NELLO: I understand what you are saying here. I received a letter this past year from a young man who attended one of our churches somewhere here in the big United States. My impression of him was that he was someone who truly loved the Lord; he was raised in church, filled with the Holy Ghost, and straight as an arrow when it came to sexual orientation. He wrote to me because of an incident that he personally experienced at his church, and he was so torn up that he had stopped attending church.

At his place of work he had befriended a coworker who just happened to be gay. As he got to know this new friend, he began to witness to him, and eventually invited him to attend church with him. The gay coworker accepted the invitation and showed up the following Sunday morning for service.

They sat together and immediately after the service was over, the pastor made a beeline back to the young saint who had invited his friend, and he asked him if his guest was gay. The young man said "yes," to which his pastor replied to him: "I don't ever want him to set foot in my church again .... gays cannot be saved, they are all going to hell, and if you allow them to come to your church, all they are going to do is destroy your church—and take your saints to hell with them."

The Best Kept Secret

NELLO: I guess when it comes to secrets, one of the best kept is that of homosexuality. Yes, it's preached against, but that's about as far as it goes. Too many preachers deny that it is in the church.

LAD: But it is. I find myself facing these issues all the time. And in my travels, I see the homosexuals in our churches, on our platforms.

NELLO: There are so many fears, Sister Doty—stigmas, gossip, rumors, mistruths, and so on, and people are just scared to death of homosexuality. They are scared of looking at those who are struggling with it, both within the church, the MIAs, and those who have never known the Lord. And so we end up with individuals all across our country, most likely in every church, struggling with homosexuality, all alone. They too keep it a secret.... and for many of the same reasons that the church keeps it a secret. You would not believe how many letters I've received from struggling individuals who say "Nello, I thought that I was the *only one* in the church who struggled with this..." And they are totally honest when they make that statement.

I hate to admit this, but I have tried to set up referrals around the country for individuals who were ready to risk making contact with one of our local pastors/churches, only to have the referral turned down. But the flipside of that is that, as I continue making these kinds of referrals, I'm finding more and more of our pastors who say "Nello, sin is sin, one is not any worse than another, and anyone who wants salvation, send them to us!" Praise God for this!

LAD: I just hate it when a group of guys—little boys or grown preachers—get together and start making their jokes. They think it makes them so tough. To me, it shows their insecurities. A strong, secure man does not have to put anybody down in order to feel good about himself, or prove to others that he is tough and straight. I don't mean to open a Pandora's Box here, but manhood can be a very fragile thing. Manhood often depends on other elements, and if any of those elements get shaky, so does the manhood. Our men have so many responsibilities. If you catch a man when one or more of these elements are on shaky ground, he can be very insecure in his manhood. I don't mean to suggest that he is some kind of latent homosexual, not by a long shot. But that weak point is when he is likely to lash out at homosexuals and independent women alike. Something is striking at his very core, and he feels threatened. Not understanding this compounds the problem.

My husband is a short Jewish man. I suppose people could make fun of him, but, as his wife, I know that God sent me a powerful man who is secure in his manhood. And I never hear him making fun of anybody. He is a man of compassion. You know, Nello, looking back on Brother Doty's life, one would conclude that he was a perfect candidate to become gay. His dad walked out on them the night he was born...he had a long series of stepfathers, none of them good, some very bad. He was raised alone by his mom, never had many playmates...I believe that what made the difference was the male mentors in his life. He had many uncles, who were his role models. Jewish families are close, and these men were there for him—going fishing, teaching him about the "guy-things." This is what we need to be doing in the church. Look around you at all the fatherless boys! Take one under your wing and show him what it's like to be a guy. Teach him those things that other little boys take for granted. Let's nip this thing in the bud!

NELLO: And don't make fun of individuals because they don't have all of the social skills and abilities you might have. Rather than making fun of a guy who can't play sports, why not go out and spend some time with him and teach him a sport? You have *no idea* what that would mean to him. Spend a day teaching him some basic auto mechanic skills. It's a very real need. I'm not saying that all gays don't know how to play sports or fix a car. There are many gays who are professional sports people and I'm sure there are gays who own an auto repair shop. But you know what I'm saying. And the same goes for the ladies..... Rather than ridicule someone who is coming out of lesbianism, go to her, share some time and teach her "how to be a lady" .... Teach her some skills.

LAD: I don't see why we have to have such a problem here. We ladies are always teaching the new converts. "...Here's a needle, honey, let's sew up that slit..." "Here's a better way to comb that hair..." and so on. Why is it so difficult to teach a former lesbian the proper ways of the godly? I'm not implying that all lesbians act like men, but whatever skills they lack, it would be pleasing to God for us to take the time to teach them, and not give in to our fears of the unknown.

Nello, do you think it is possible that this very lack of opportunity to learn these kinds of skills actually plays right into Satan's hideous scheme to deceive our precious young people?

NELLO: Yes, I do. I remember one of the most traumatic events in my youth.... an event that impacted the rest of my life, and was used to build more of the homosexual *lie* into the fabric of my own life. One day, not long after I first started school, we went out for recess. All of us boys headed off to play some baseball. Now I had never played baseball in my life. Hey, never had anyone to teach me. And while I didn't have a clue of how to play or what the rules were, at that point I was not scared. I was excited and having a blast ... I was learning a new game.

So it came my turn to bat.... now keep in mind that I had never even held a bat in my hands.... But there I go, up to the plate.... the ball is thrown, and I'm telling you, I connected with that ball, and if ever a ball was hit out of the "stadium," I hit that ball out of the park. Now this all sounds good... so far.

So I started running around the bases..... First, second, third, and then—home! I had scored a home run! All of my team was cheering me.... Wow! ...... And then! I looked and saw that the ball was still so far out and knew that I could run around the bases again and score another home run!

Need I say more...? I didn't make it. And I was called out, and the first home run was not allowed. I was laughed at, made fun of... Never was I so humiliated... in fact, I don't think I've ever shared this story with anyone until right now....

As a result of what happened that day, I never again even got close to sports ... I was scared to death to try any sport.... there was actual panic. I would see sports being played, and I would want to join in, but from that day on, I never did. And what all of that did was just create more "different" for me, more separation from what I "should have been"... One thing leading to another, to another, to another...

LAD: Oh my! I wonder what would have happened—that old proverbial "what if?"—had the coach been more sensitive—more of a leader and less of a judge. What if he had taken the time to teach you the rules? Your life might have gone in a completely different

59

direction. That is a lesson for all of us—let's keep our eyes on the little kids. Let's watch for those who lack social skills and athletic skills. Take them aside and teach them how.

I've heard of boys who became terrified of team sports because they had a physical abnormality that had not yet been diagnosed. One child's depth perception was so far off that he kept bumping into the other kids during a volleyball game. They mocked him right off the court. Later, when his problem was diagnosed, it was too late. His fears were too real. By then, he was labeled ugly names because he stayed away from sports.

NELLO: Historically, the church has not had a very good track record of reaching out to gays. The purpose of the church is to be there for all sinners, and we should have been there for gays as well. We should have been actively ministering to, reaching out to, bringing in, the gays and lesbians. But those that were in the church were run off, and those that had not yet made it in to the church, found the church doors shut to them. If we wouldn't take them in, where could they go?

LAD: We need to be there for the sinners and also for each other. We need to treat our brothers and sisters right—with love. The homosexual community stands ready to take our people in and treat them good. Stephen had church people lie to him, cheat him, stab him in the back, and refuse him help when he needed it. In contrast to that, was the gay community bending over backwards—especially during the early stages—to be helpful and supportive. We need to be helpful and kind to each other. The church is a family and, unfortunately, family has a way of hurting each other as nobody else can.

NELLO: In years gone by, other sins were just as looked down on.... alcoholism, drugs, prostitution, unwed mothers, and so on. But thank the Lord, take a look today at what's happened in our church.... Rather than shutting these sinners out, we now have actual programs in place for them. We are now able to be there for them, watching and helping them as the Lord cleans them up, sets them free.

LAD: I know a lady who was a pitiful alcoholic. She was invited to a crusade in a California city, and was told that the evangelist would help her find deliverance. She wanted to go so bad, but the fears kept growing, and she drank herself into a real state. When time came to go to the meeting, they had to hold her up and slip her in the back door. The evangelist happened to look up as she came in, and the Lord spoke to him, "I am going to deliver that lady tonight." And sure enough, during the altar service, God did it. The evangelist went over to her and asked if she wanted to be set free of alcohol. When she said Yes, he explained that when he would lay his hand on her head, all desire to drink would leave her then and there. Well, it did, and she's never wanted another drink. I would like to see more of that in our churches. I think too often we are afraid of stepping out on faith for God. But it's His reputation on the line, not ours. God wants to do so much—and would, if we would just let Him.

God delivered me from alcohol immediately when He gave me His Spirit. We can have that! It does not have to be long and drawn out, week after week of "working the steps." I realize that sometimes that can be part of His plan, too. But I deeply feel that God wants to do the miracles and deliverances, but we, His people, are too afraid. But until we can get past that, churches are getting programs in place now to work with people.

NELLO: And now we have another group of sinners— homosexuals—that need the same thing.... I know that change is already starting to happen....I know that we now have more and more churches and pastors who are willing to minister to gays.

LAD: I have been praying for that, for ten years so far—and it has been a lonely ten years because there were so few people I could talk to about my pain and confusion.

NELLO: And probably nobody in the truth. I am thankful, too, Sister Doty, that more churches are opening up. But they are still keeping it "low keyed".... some pastors are afraid of what others will say, what their members will say... it's sort of like they will work with the gay struggler and say, "Let's get you all cleaned up for the Lord, but we better keep your past a secret." And sadly, we still have those that have their church doors bolted shut to the gay struggler. But change is happening; it's happening today, and the Lord is opening the doors wide!

LAD: What are your feelings about that, Nello—about keeping the past a secret? I know Satan loves secrets. When we keep secrets hidden in the dark, he can wreak havoc with them. He uses them to bind, to accuse, to threaten, to tear down what God has done. Over and over, as I deal with hurting people, I find that the first key is getting that secret out of the murky darkness and into the light. It's rather like a wound on the skin. There is a time to keep it covered, bandaged up. But there comes a time when we must expose it to the sun (Son) so it will heal.

I think that one of the reasons some of our twelve-step programs work is the concept of sponsorship—reaching out to mentor others. They invest in others' lives. They step out and care. But this comes only after recognizing their own problem and speaking it out.

NELLO: Rather than keep it a secret, and hiding what the Lord is doing in these people's lives, these testimonies need to be shared. The more people standing up to testify to what the Lord has done, the more those who are struggling will start reaching out and receiving the help and the support that they desperately need from their pastors and from their church.

I heard something a long time ago from a minister who came out of homosexuality and is now working with the black churches in reaching out to gays. He used Lazarus as an example of a sinner coming to the Lord.... and specifically, a homosexual coming to the Lord. He talked about Lazarus being "dead"..... all wrapped up in the tomb gauze, buried, in the grave .... And then the Lord shows up, and brings Lazarus *back to life*! But then what happened.... as Lazarus made his way out of the tomb, was he "free?" No, he was still all bound up with the wrappings and cloth and all of that stuff..... So here he comes, stumbling all around, bumping into everything, having one hard time ... and what did the Lord have to say to His disciples.... He said: "Loose him, and let him go!" What is suggested here is that ONLY the Lord can bring us who were dead in sin, back to life: .... but then, it's the work of the church to touch them, to help them get loose of all that had them bound. This was so powerful for me.

LAD: I received a letter myself, recently. This young man said, "Thank you so much for writing HELP ME HEAL. It made me feel less alone. God has now delivered me, and I want to reach out to others in this lifestyle. In the churches, Sister Doty, people—especially men, in my case—tend to shy away from those like me. They distance themselves, and I've ended up in situations of being at a social gathering, surrounded by happy laughing people, and feeling so alone."

NELLO: One of the big reasons that people in the church will not reach out to homosexuals is the fear that if they do, if they are seen with a gay person, then people will think they are also gay. A very dear friend of mine (he was there for me as I made my way to the Lord and he led me, guided me, supported me, prayed for me, just loved me, and he's my best buddy today) shared with me something that he experienced that we still laugh about. When he was first working with me, he was at a bookstore and just happened to see a book that he thought might be of help to me. He pulled it off of the shelf, continued his shopping, and then headed to the cashier. He then looked at the book that he was going to buy for me, and when he saw the word "homosexuality" on the cover, he became scared that the cashier would think that he was gay. He could not bring himself to purchase the book. So he put it back on the shelf and went home and ordered the book for me off the Internet! That was a real eye opener for him and we talked about it and we still laugh about it today.

Another reason that some in our churches will not reach out to homosexuals, is that they, or someone close to them, may have had a very negative experience, like being molested by a gay person. As a result, they ended up with anger, resentment, and downright hatred, toward all gays. Now this is tragic on several fronts. Even if a gay person tried to reach out to them for help, they would reject them, kick them out. It is also tragic that as long as they continue to carry that hate, they themselves are in jeopardy of losing out with the Lord; the other tragic part is that they spread their anger and hate to others in the church, especially if they are in a leadership position. Yes, what might have happened to them or a family member is tragic, and it should never have happened, and it's normal to feel the anger, but—like it or not, at some point we are going to have to forgive, or we ourselves will be destroyed.

LAD: You got that right! Forgiveness is a huge issue in the church! Nello, I am constantly working with hurting people, and the majority of the time, we uncover the matter of unforgiveness. In their past lurks some horrible issue. A person or persons have hurt them terribly, and they will not forgive.

At the same time, too, I feel that there's a whole lot of forgiveness that needs to be done on the homosexual's part. Many of them have been hurt badly, and are carrying grudges you wouldn't believe. Somehow, some way, they have got to reach the point of letting go of it. What was once a root of bitterness will take hold and grow into a huge, ugly monster that they will take with them to the grave if they aren't willing to forgive.

My own brother was treated very badly by his first wife. And he refused to let go of it. I talked to him not too long before his death. I tried to explain the necessity of letting go of this hurt. "I'll never forgive her," he told me. As far as I know, he never did. What a waste, what a tragic waste.

My Stephen has a lot to let go of. I pray daily that God will grant forgiveness to him, and fill his heart with forgiveness for those who hurt him.

The Music Department

While working on this book, I asked several music directors for their opinions on the connection between homosexuality and music. The church has lost an inordinate number of musicians to homosexuality. One music director told me this:

> Music was made for worship to God. God must love music because he made it for Himself. Music has many traits such as: easy, soft, beautiful, loose, free-flowing, graceful, pretty, emotional, and colorful. And when people use music for reasons other than the worship of God, the traits of music become a part of the person instead of the purpose of the music. They become selfish, just as Lucifer became selfish as being the chief musician of heaven. He lost his focus for the purpose of music and sought glory for himself. He became a self-worshipper.
>
> More than just the music itself, I believe it relates to the undue praise and glory that musicians acquire before an audience. There is an appetite developed for glory. This leads to a self-love or self-worship, which is the ultimate selfishness. The spirit of homosexuality is very acquainted with the traits of music. And if music is used for any other purpose than worship to God, that spirit will attach itself to that person. I believe that it is easier for these spirits to attach themselves to musicians because musicians

have to be open-spirited and free-minded. I think that people who are unaware of the dangers of music are most susceptible to this spirit. I also believe that Satan has a particular interest in musicians just because of his own past."

I was also curious as to why our women musicians are not falling into homosexuality. I asked this music director for this thoughts:

I know this is a very simplistic answer to a very complex question. I believe that, if everything has a feminine and masculine side, music leans heavily toward the feminine side (of course this has much qualification to be said). The traits of music, and the fact that you somewhat "give in to" music as a musician, places the woman in her rightful place. Whereas for men, if the bounds are overtaken, it puts him in his unrightful place. The bounds being anything other than for the pure submission to God in music. Some women may be just as guilty as the man who does this; however, the result is not homosexuality, because she is not going against her nature. It can however, result in adultery or other sin.

From these comments, I would like to caution our musicians— please keep your focus on God with your music. It would appear to me that the same anointing that once rested upon Lucifer before his fall, is still alive in the world today. Lucifer does not want to let go of it, and when he spots it in someone else, he will attempt to take control of it.

7
Words to Friends and Family

We are living in the end time, and as in the day of Sodom, so shall the coming of the Son of Man be. The spirit of homosexuality has been unleashed on the earth as never before. It is a powerful spirit. It is a very real spirit. We will be seeing it more and more in our churches, but as we learned in Chapter Five, it will usher in a far worse evil. Hiding our heads in the sand will not make the problem go away. In my work as counselor, I'm continually being confronted with the knowledge that yet another brother, sometimes a sister, is gay. Take Althea.

Althea's day began just like any other day. Up at six, breakfast for Bill and the kids, get them off to school and work, and Althea sank into the easy chair by the window for her daily devotions. Her heart was light this morning. It was storming and cold outside but, inside, by the light of the soft lamp, Althea felt snug and warm. She was content with her life, happy with the Lord and with her family. She was not prepared that morning for the beginning of the end of her beautiful world.

As she completed her devotions and was placing her Bible on the end table, she saw it. A piece of paper or something behind Bill's recliner, across from hers. With a smile at her husband's carelessness, she reached behind his chair to retrieve—a photograph. Althea gasped. A young man clad in a bikini, smiling into the camera. Tanned, white teeth, muscular. She frowned. Who was this? What was Bill doing with this picture?

Before dinner that night, Althea knew. As she held the picture out to him, Bill confessed to her. He was homosexual. He had struggled for years, he said, and for the past six months, had at last become a practicing homosexual. He felt it would be best if they divorced. Althea felt heat, cold, and dizziness all at the same time. Where had she gone wrong?

☐

Marvin's wife Marianne left him for another companion, a female she met on the internet. He had wondered about Marianne spending so many hours on the computer. Marvin, a minister of the gospel, was haunted by the question: where had he gone wrong?

☐

Suzanne's handsome young son announced to her one afternoon, "Mom, I guess you'd better hear it from me than someone else. I'm gay." Suzanne was devastated. Her child? Her own flesh and blood? She cried out to God in the darkness of the night, "Where did I go wrong?"

☐

All of these people were tormented by fears and imaginations about what they had done to contribute to this. You will notice a particular question each of them asked: "Where did I go wrong?" What could they have done differently?

I could not count the nights I cried myself to sleep after Stephen left. I cried to God, telling Him all about my failures and asked Him— please, Lord!—to somehow make it all up to my son and bring him back. The guilt (some false, some real) consumed me for a long time. Guilt melted into shame, and then into anger. Angry at myself—why didn't I pray more? Why didn't I see it coming? How could I have missed the signs? Angry at Stephen—how could he be so stupid? Why did he throw everything away, and for what? But mostly angry at the devil—how dare he steal my son with his filth and his lies! Only another mother who has lost her child to homosexuality could begin to understand this particular kind of pain.

The next phase I passed through was denial—Stephen wouldn't really sin, he was a good boy. He really was. I went through a period of hating every homosexual I saw—somehow I blamed them, perfect strangers, for deceiving and defiling my son. I could not accept this—I would not! If I denied it long enough, surely I would wake up and find it was all just a horrible dream.

One mother cried in my arms. "Was I too domineering?" she sobbed. "I've heard that domineering mothers make homosexual boys." But most of the men I've dealt with, either directly or through their mothers, were boys who had been raised with father problems, not mother problems. Either the father was absent physically, or he was absent emotionally. When a boy's father is there for him, he does not have this kind of identity problem. He has the security of a father who cares, who models, and who gives him a sense of belonging. A father who does not provide for those of his own household is worse than an infidel. Provision means a whole lot more than just paying the bills. Fathers must provide emotionally, spiritually, and mentally for their children. Failing to do so sets the children up for the enemy's camp. If dad won't give what his child needs, Satan will be more than happy to provide a counterfeit somewhere along the line! Can we really think that it is a coincidence that the number of fatherless homes has soared along with the rate of homosexuality?

Boys with absent fathers can be desperately searching for a father's love. A father happens to be male. They are searching for an identity. They grow up, often surrounded by females, and therefore become more familiar with the female than the male. In the normal pattern of maturing, girls gravitate to girls for intimate friendship and hanging out, and the same for boys. Girls are familiar with girls, and boys are familiar with boys. Girls play dolls together, and boys play army. Girls do like mama, and boys follow after dad. This is the way things are meant to be. God created the two-parent family—not out of whim, but because it is what makes things work right. It is part of His wonderful plan.

So when the boy and girl grow up and it becomes time to date, they are attracted to that which is different, not so familiar. The girl seeks the boy; the boy seeks the girl.

But when there is no father for the boy to love and be close to, he seeks it from mama and sisters, and maybe sister's girlfriends. Girls become familiar. He becomes much more comfortable with girls as friends than boys. But when it becomes time for him to begin to date, seek out a mate, he is drawn to the unfamiliar. In his case, that would be the male.

I'm not trying to be hard on the daddies. Many fathers truly love their little sons, but just don't know how to show it. Many of them feel that by working sixteen-hour days and providing materially, they are showing their love. Many of them—as in the case of Stephen's father—just walked away. My first husband did not walk away from Stephen; he walked away from *me*. He told me many times in those final months together that, as long as the children were with me, he would never have to worry about them...and since I had a "bright and prosperous" future ahead as a clinical psychologist, he did not have to worry about us financially. That is no excuse, and Stephen realizes that, and it hurts. The absent father cannot wrap his arms around his little boy and hold him close. He is not there to comfort...to train...to nurture...to fulfill that need of every little boy to be held by daddy.

Stephen never complained. He was not a whiner. He seemed to accept the loss of his dad. But recently there has been a tremendous need to find out about him—what happened to him? Where did he disappear? Was he dead or alive? Stephen searched the Internet, returned to his birthplace, but discovered nothing. No news. No information. No closure. I pray that he will soon be able to settle this in his heart; it would mean so much to him.

When You Learn That (S)He is Gay...

Following are some tips I have gleaned and that I feel might be of help to you.

1. First of all, be calm! Although it might seem that God has lost control, He has not. Nothing takes God by surprise, and He knew about this long before you did. So do your best to remain calm. When you first learn that a loved one is homosexual, that is not the time to try to deal with your own feelings of insecurity and fear. Try to focus on what he or she is needing from you at this particular moment. This will set the trend for some time to come, and you want the communication lines kept open.

Count to ten, walk around the block, but do not vent your anger. Remember, whatever you're feeling is normal for you. Don't be critical of your feelings of anger and helplessness and wanting to strike out. You are experiencing a true loss, and can expect to go through the usual stages of grief—shock and disbelief, denial, anger, pain, depression. Try to flow with it, accepting that it is normal under the circumstances. You have just been dealt an awful blow.

2. Don't preach and lecture. They have already told themselves anything you might tell them. They have already struggled and fought and had countless conversations inside their heads. You can't add anything new at this point. By the time you discover your loved one is gay, he has already lived through all the torments. They don't need your lectures and certainly not your harshness

3. Give your person unconditional love. Instantly, your beloved husband or child has become a stranger to you. But he is still your

loved one. Love him with no strings attached. Your love is vital at this point—it is truly his lifeline back to God. Don't let him feel that you are rejecting him when he needs you most. Acceptance is not the same as approval. You accept the person, but this does not mean you are accepting homosexuality. God hates the sin; it is an abomination to Him. But always, He loves the homosexual. Someone asked me recently if this wasn't somehow a contradiction, or hypocritical. I asked this person, do you stop loving the alcoholic (her husband, in this case) because he is alcoholic? No, she replied. She loved him. But she sure hated the alcoholism. It's the same thing.

4. Later, after you have assured them of your love and support, and when you are calm, you might talk to them about it. But don't beat them over the head with Bible verses and information! Don't preach. Just gently, with love and compassion, remind them that homosexuality is a sin; it is a lifestyle that grieves God. Let them know that you love them and will support them, and that you will always be there for them. But you must let them know, too, that you cannot condone the sin.

5. Give them hope! Hold out an alternative for them. Let them know that the love and the power of Jesus Christ can redeem and recreate them. Try to hook up with an ex-gay ministry, such as Beacon Ministries, so you can provide something concrete for them. A phone number, a brochure, a tape, a website.

Settle In for the Ride

So far, so good. But unfortunately, all of this is just the beginning for you. Once you learn the truth—once you have regained your composure and have begun to look to Jesus for help—once you have communicated your love and support—once you have placed a spark of hope in their soul—you are then in for the long journey! You will need support, also. The homosexual lifestyle is one filled with instability, broken promises, lies, and shattered hearts. You can provide a listening ear, a place of warmth, security and wholesomeness that sin will never be able to offer your loved one. But you yourself must have a strong emotional support system. Confide in your pastor or one or two close friends. Check to see if there is a local Christian support group for spouses or parents of gays. There is real strength in learning that you are not alone in this! Satan's tool, as always, is to isolate you, make you feel you are the only one in the world going through this. You are not alone! God is with you and for you. And He has provided you with a network support system somewhere. Seek it out and use it.

One of the hardest things you might have to bear is the reaction of friends, family, and the church itself. Homosexuality seems to bring out the worst in people. Fear. Repulsion. Anger. These are typical reactions, but they are also hurtful and emotional, and the church needs to get a handle on this.

In those times when the anger and sorrow seem overwhelming, try to remember not to take it personally. Try to look at their homosexuality as a fact. This is just the way it is. It is not something intended to hurt you. It is not a statement of your failure, or your value. Homosexuality is a complicated thing. There is not one single factor that causes it, but a whole array of contributing factors. Parents, especially, are vulnerable at this point. Cuddle up to Jesus, and refuse to listen to the lies of the devil.

Stephen has never once blamed me. When I contacted him to get his permission to write about him in this book, our lines of communication on this issue began to open up. He told me this: "I think it's important that you mention in your book some of the things about growing up, about school... having an aversion to sports and P.E. and being constantly picked on and called ugly names throughout my teens—yes, even church boys and girls did it—so could it be possible that all this was additional influence?"

The point here is that it is not just one thing that causes homosexuality. It's not just Daddy. It's not just Mama. It's not just the sports issue, or the name-calling. Self-condemnation is not going to do any good, so let go of it. You must give it all to God. There probably *were* mistakes made. But those mistakes alone did not create this condition. Also, if God knows everything—the beginning and the ending (which He does)—then He knew in advance the mistakes you were going to make. And He made provision for them in advance! God works even our mistakes out for good! Cling to this promise (Romans 8:28)!

Special Kind of Prayer

Praying for your homosexual can be quite an experience. There will be times when you feel so dry. You have prayed every prayer there is to pray. You have asked everything of God you can think of. It is at this point that parents and wives, especially, can be tricked into feeling false guilt by the enemy. I reached a point in my prayers for Stephen that I just didn't have anything left to say. I felt terribly guilty! And then my friend Janice would remind me that prayer is like breathing out and breathing in...ebb and flow.... God and Mama, passing the burden back and forth—Mama working on it with prayer, then God working on it. Back and forth. Breathe in and breathe out. Burdens were never meant to be carried 24/7.

Then there were times when I would lie face down on my living room rug at three in the morning, crying out for God to forgive me for whatever it was I might have done that caused my son to go this way. In those times, we need to remember that, when God convicts us, He will tell us what we have done wrong. That kind of "free-floating guilt" is from the enemy. I hate to think of all the hours I spent doing that kind of groveling when I could have been praying warfare prayers.

One of the hard prayers that we must pray is that, if our loved one is hiding sin, he will be caught. It must be revealed, brought out of the darkness so he can repent. The homosexual confusion usually lies dormant inside the person. God cannot allow sin into heaven; so He allows it to come out now so that the person can be cleansed and healed and made whole. As long as he is going to church and everything looks all right on the surface, how would you know to pray about this particular problem? I didn't. Thank God that it is out in the open, and ask Him for direction in how to pray.

Our Theme Song

I was listening to a song the other night that said, "Fight until you can't fight any longer. Then get up and fight some more." This is the theme song for the person with a gay loved one. There will be times you feel like giving up. These are the times you must hang on with all your might. Hang onto God. It is then that He will most certainly fight this battle for you. Stand still, Mama, and see the salvation of the Lord! Stand still, Wife, and watch God work! He is still on the throne. He is still in control. The battle is not yours, but the Lord's. Never give up! My husband always teaches that, if you give up and stop praying, it is very possible that the very next prayer you would have prayed would have been the one that brought the answer. Keep on praying.

There will be times when circumstances scream, "It's no use! He's gone off the deep end this time!" Those are the times, dear one, to rest in God. Mark 11:22 tells us to "Have faith in God." Not in our prayers, not in our fasting, not in our loved one's great personality—but simply, have faith in God. There are so many times I feel like I am hanging on by my fingernails and ready to slip. But He is faithful. He is always there. Sometimes it is not until we have absolutely come to the end of ourselves that God can be assured He will get the glory for it. It is not until we have done everything we know to do to get our child saved—and we have failed. Then we will know it was truly God.

Not too long after Stephen left, I asked a friend how much she prayed for her MIAs. She told me this, and I've never forgotten it: "I'm afraid I don't do a whole lot of praying. Mostly I just cry." God hears our cries! He sees our broken hearts! And when my friend's children return to the Lord, she will know it was God and God alone!

There will be times when you cry out, "God, I've prayed for everything I can think of. There's nothing left for me to pray!" That is when you start all over and keep praying. Remember the unjust judge. God will honor your prayers if you pray, believing. Sooner or later, you'll receive an assurance that He has heard and answered your prayer. From that point on, your job is simply to praise and thank Him for a job well done (although you have not yet seen it!).

The Power of Praise

You must learn to praise as never before. What I mean by that is you will need more than just the words, "Praise the Lord," or "Praise You, Jesus." You will have to get yourself so focused on God and His absolute power, that His mighty acts and ways become a part of you. Be filled with thanksgiving. Learn to delight yourself in the Lord. His promise is to give you the desires of your heart if you will delight yourself in Him. Somebody needs to write a book: "Enjoying Jesus!" Trust Him. Leave your loved one in His hands. Give God the honor and the praise for still being in control. If your loved one has been washed in the blood, then he is God's property. God will redeem him. But you must believe God.

There will be times when the last thing on earth you want to do is praise. Your flesh recoils at the very thought of it. You are weary, worn out, and discouraged—maybe even a little miffed at God. But the Bible calls for the sacrifice of praise. It is easy to praise when we feel like it—and you know all this. It is much harder—but, I believe, much more effectual—to praise when it is a sacrifice. I believe God really sits up and takes notice when we do that. He says, "That's my child there, believing in Me, even though her whole world is shattered. I'm going to get in there and do something about this." The best sacrifice hurts. We forget that no one knows about sacrifices better than our Lord!

I remember times when, just as I began to see improvement in Stephen, and it seemed he was on his way back to God—he would go off on some other sinful adventure. And I would be devastated. I felt like I lived on a wild roller coaster ride. I wanted it to stop so I could get off, but it just kept on going and going. The frustration would cut me so very deep. Often, it would lead to anger. There are still these times when I'm certain that any moment now, he will be back in the fold, and he does not. But I have learned that it is in God's timing. I believe that He will save the son of His handmaid (Psalm 86:16). I cannot tell God WHEN. I cannot tell God HOW. It is my job just to quietly wait and see the salvation of the Lord.

Calling all Mothers!

Mothers who long for support—for others who understand what you are going through—let's band together. Let's form a powerful prayer network! E-mail Sister Doty at director@awpministries.org. You can also go to my website, www.awpministries.org or the Parents Support page of www.beaconministries.net. Together, we can make a difference!

Parts of the above were excerpted from my book, HELP ME HEAL, available from Pentecostal Publishing House, 8855 Dunn Road, Hazelwood, MO 63042, 314-837-7300, or see order form on the last page of this book.

8
What Do Gays Need to Hear?

Individuals struggling with homosexuality, either in or out of the church, need to hear first and foremost, that there is hope for them. They were NOT born that way; it is NOT in their genes. They need to hear that, as others have escaped that lifestyle, so can they. They need to hear that they are NOT alone..... that thousands of others struggle with the same battle. They need to hear that it affects our church on every level, from members to every position of leadership, including pastors; that it's in every one of our Bible colleges, and that the others, just like them, are keeping the old secret going. There is a HUGE relief to the individual once they know that it's not JUST them.

LAD: I can relate to that. I've had some secrets in my own past that brought me much shame—and the deepest shame was imagining that no one else had ever experienced the things I did. When I learned otherwise, it was like a breath of fresh air—not that I enjoyed knowing about their hurt and pain. I was not happy that they hurt. But just knowing that others shared in this was liberating! Satan loses his power. I've been criticized for being too honest and transparent in my books, but that is one of the things that has helped people. They see that others have been where they are—with the same kinds of secret pains—and that, if God did it for me, He will also do it for them. I am not saying that people have to "let it all hang out," you know, their dirty laundry sort of thing. This is not about that. This is about spiritual warfare, because it removes a very powerful weapon from our enemy, disarms him. I absolutely refuse to let him intimidate me with mistakes from my past. They are under the blood, and out of his control.

NELLO: There you go! They also need to hear that there are others who, like them, have struggled with homosexuality, *and* received the strength from the Lord to fight that battle. They need to hear that there are now individuals who are at last standing up and giving God the Glory for freedom from homosexuality. They need to hear that regardless of how they may have been treated by churches in the past, we do have pastors and churches now that offer support. They need this message of HOPE loud and clear, and they need to be able to see and hear from others who have experienced this.

LAD: Like the boy I mentioned in HELP ME HEAL...if they could just know that there are people walking in truth, living for God...who knew and *understood* their struggles.

NELLO: Right! And something else they need to hear—something very important—is that just because they might have a thought that could lead to sin does not mean that they have sinned. They need to know that when thoughts or old memories pop into their head, that in and of itself is not sin. It is not a sin to be tempted. They need to know that it's when they decide to hold on to that thought and to entertain it—that is when they move into the arena of sin.

It can be very difficult to break our thought patterns, but people do it everyday. They must cast down all of those imaginations. They must allow the Lord to clean out all of the chambers of their minds, and He *will*. As they grow closer to the Lord, they become more willing to allow Him into all their secret rooms. They need to know that when the old thoughts hit, they *do have a choice* to rebuke it, to call upon the Lord for strength and a way of escape. Refusing to allow those old ugly thoughts entrance into our minds gives us a good feeling of well-being. We are taking control of our lives again!

LAD: In my seminar, "The Power of Godly Thinking," people learn to say—out loud so the devil can hear them, too—"I refuse that thought!" I don't care if it's sexual sins, or jealousy, or fear—we must learn to control our thinking. Refuse that thought! Don't dwell on it! Refuse to entertain it! God may be standing in the shadows somewhere, just watching—waiting—and as soon as He knows you mean business, He will step in and help.

Yes, when we have indulged in the habit of allowing our minds free rein over the years, it is hard to break that habit. But it can be broken, and be broken it must! What has happened is that we allow strongholds to be built in our minds. When I lived in Nebraska, there was a spot on my front porch where a mama bird started building a nest. I would watch her as bit by bit, she brought the materials in and built this nest. Fascinating!

After the babies had come and gone and there was no other need for that nest, my husband took it down. I held it in my hands, amazed at how tight it was. That mama had built a nest so strong that no harm could get to her babies. All those little twigs—normally easily broken or carried away by the wind—formed a mighty strong little fortress. That's how it is with our thought patterns. Over the years, we have added a thought (twig) here and a thought (twig) there, until we end up with a powerful and mighty fortress within our minds! That is what I call a stronghold. It must be torn down. Destroyed. The same way it was built—twig by twig—thought by thought—until it is no longer a stronghold. The Lord will help you if you are serious about it.

Some thoughts are harder than others to resist. Some we just seem to enjoy more. We need to find a strong motivation, one that is stronger than the enjoyment. Just knowing that the Lord is displeased can be enough. You see, He knows our every thought. We might be able to hide them from everybody else. No one else might ever suspect the slimy, stinking garbage inside our minds. But our Lord knows. And He deeply cares. He longs for us to have clean and pure minds. David cried out, *"Create in me a clean heart, O Lord!"* (Psalm 51:10) That should be our prayer every day. I pray it often. I long for a clean heart.

NELLO: They need to hear about shame and its connection with keeping their struggle a secret.... how secrets are used by the enemy to keep the shame alive...how shame binds, how it paralyzes.... and that's just one part of why the church has got to stand up to its responsibilities. All sinners need to feel safe in reaching out to their pastor, to their brothers and sisters. And as soon as the secret is out, the power of the shame is destroyed. It can't be used against them any more. Also, we don't get the prayers and support of others when we keep it a secret. So at some point the struggling homosexual must be able to feel safe enough to reach out and to share his struggles with someone else. Man, what a relief it was that day that the words came out of my mouth that I was gay.... and when I received God's love and compassion back from a brother in church, BOOM! The chains were destroyed.

LAD: A sister came to me just recently and started telling me how she had been a lesbian for years, and how God had delivered her when she received the Holy Ghost. All desire gone, just like that! And no one knows about it, she has kept it secret. As she was talking to me, her face took on an absolute glow. She grew more and more radiant as her story tumbled out. And she said, "Oh, it feels so *good*, just talking about it!"

Something else you just said really touched me, Nello. Secrets cannot receive support and prayer. I kept Stephen's secret for several years. I kept thinking, if no one knows, it will make it easier for him to come back to God. I wonder now, how many prayers for him could have been prayed, and were not, because of my misguided secret. All along, I thought I was doing the right thing, the best thing for him...paving the way for his return.

NELLO: People keeping secrets usually do feel it's the best thing to do, Sister Doty. But Stephen and all the rest need to hear that Christians who truly love the Lord and are truly serving the Lord do love them ... not the sin, not any sin, but that they will be there for them. Just as important is that they also hear that there will always be those who will not reach out to them; we will always have the hypocrites, the self righteous ones..... so they need to make up their minds that they are in this for themselves and to serve the Lord, and that no matter what another "jerk" has to say, they will pray for that person rather than let the enemy use it to push them out of God's will and love. They need to know that it's not for them to judge the hypocrites, that's God's job, but they need to know that the Lord will hold us responsible when we hurt another person. I would hate to stand in their shoes on Judgment Day. They need to hear that the Lord loves them, has always loved them, and that He has the only real answer, the only real path out of homosexuality.

LAD: You know, Nello, I've always heard it said that God loves us just the way we are...but He loves us too much to allow us to remain this way! Thank God for God! That's how He is with this sin of homosexuality! Any homosexual can come to God, just as he is. And God will receive him, and love him. But God loves that person far too much to let him remain in that sin. Isn't that another way of saying, "Hate the sin but love the sinner?" Oh, to be loved by God! How awesome it is! But what I really prefer to tell someone is that I love the sinner and hate anything that hurts him—and sin hurts him!

NELLO: And that is something else they need to hear, Sister Doty. They need to hear "seek ye first the kingdom of God and then..." The message out there is that the gay person has got to rid themselves of all the "trimmings" that they have accumulated in their life of homosexuality *before* they can walk through the church door, before they can come to the Lord for repentance, forgiveness, and true salvation. The church is for sinners..... That's where they are supposed to come. But again, they have so many fears—fears of rejection, being made fun of, talked about—and the enemy uses this against them to prevent them from walking through our church doors. And granted, many of their fears are legitimate.

They need to hear that they don't necessarily get "fixed" first. As they take their first baby steps toward the Lord and freedom from homosexuality, their focus needs to be on drawing closer to Him. They need to focus on building a strong personal relationship with the Lord. Then, as they grow stronger in the Lord, they begin to experience the freedom they are looking for. Now none of this means that they just go out and continue sinning, and this does not mean that the Lord can't give instant freedom—deliverance—from any sin because He does.

They need to hear that when they stumble, when they slip, make a mistake, they must *always get right back up.* Now the enemy loves it when we slip up.... he points that old talon and says "See, you can't do it, see, there is no hope." Or he says, "Well, since you slipped, you might as well just go out and get your fill and then repent later..." What a bunch of lies. No, the person needs to learn that no matter if they slip twenty times in one day, they must repent and get back up twenty times!

LAD: Sometimes it is very difficult to grasp the fact that God is truly on our side. He loves us, He is pulling for us, and He longs to see us succeed! Hebrews 12:1 talks about a great cloud of witnesses. This is a beautiful passage of scripture. In the chapter just before this—the famous "Hall of Faith" chapter—the author names many who won a place in this special Hall. He also mentioned many whose names were *not* listed. The point here is: as we fight in this war—and as we run in this race—we are surrounded by this great cloud of witnesses—and they, like God, are cheering us on. "Come on, you can do it! You can make it! If I can do it," they seem to be yelling, "so can you!" When you are part of the family of God, you have a lot of people rooting for you. You will have battles, but you can win! God will always deliver the righteous!

NELLO: Yes, they need to understand that—until we meet the Lord—we are always going to have battles of one sort or another. Pride is a big one we will always have to fight. Bro. T.F. Tenney made the statement that "Probably if we totem-poled sin, we would put homosexuality up at the top and pride at the bottom...I doubt if God would....He would probably put pride at the top....After all, that is what got Lucifer....Sin is Sin." (Pentecostal Herald, June, 2000, p.18)

LAD: Good for Brother Tenney! I know all sin will keep us out of heaven, and God hates it all. But you know something—and this will probably cause some reading this book to throw it down—I personally believe that *pride* is worse than homosexuality, because if it weren't for pride, there would be no homosexuality. Out of pride comes Self. If it weren't for pride, there would be no sin, period. What do we think caused Lucifer to get kicked out of heaven—making passes at the other angels?

Pride is the original sin—not the actual eating of the fruit. If Eve had not wanted to satisfy Self, and to be as smart as God, she would not have eaten the fruit. Pride was there first. Of course she could have refused to eat the fruit. It shows the importance of our thoughts, Nello. Eve stopped at that forbidden tree and looked. While she was looking, she was thinking. If only she had nipped it in the bud right then and there! If only she had attended a seminar on The Power of Godly Thinking!

When she first paused at the tree, it was probably just normal curiosity. If the devil hadn't come along at just that moment, it might have been okay. (I would not be surprised if he had taken up sentry at that particular spot, just waiting for the right moment.) But he appealed to her pride. I heard something really good the other day—a definition of "ego." It means, "Edging God Out." We have to watch out for pride. Pray it out of our lives. We cannot afford to let it in, because it will kill us every time. It is very deceptive, and very lethal.

"The" Spirit

People struggling with gay desires usually find that gays everywhere are approaching them. They seem to come out of the woodwork. There might be 50 other people in the room, but the lesbian seems to make a beeline for you; the gay spots you in the biggest crowd. Why is that? How do these gays know?

I almost hate to mention the "spirit of homosexuality," because some people will want to blame everything on that. But it is a very real spirit. And you can do something about it. You do not have to receive and accept and entertain it. You can kick it out!

The reason gays can spot you a mile away is because of that spirit. That spirit with them recognizes that spirit hovering around you. There is a lot taking place in the supernatural that we cannot see. But it is every bit as real as the shoes on your feet or the watch on your wrist. This is also why child abusers are drawn to children with a history of abuse. Battered women just naturally attract the batterers. One rape victim told me that it was like she wore a big magnetic sign saying, "Rape Me." This is because of the spirits we just mentioned.

But the good news with all of this is that, if we are born again of the water and the Spirit, we have the power (Acts 1:8) to command, in the name of Jesus, that these spirits depart from us. Probably some of the toughest spirits we've ever heard about were with the man who lived in the tombs of the Gadarenes (See Mark 5 and Luke 8). Tough! And yet Jesus cast out these ungodly spirits, and the man was made whole.

But that was Jesus! you protest. The ordinary saint cannot do that. But that is not what the Word says. In John 14:12-13, Jesus promises: *Verily, verily, I say unto you, He that believeth on me, the works that I do shall he do also; and greater works than these shall he do; because I go unto my Father. And whatsoever ye shall ask in my name, that will I do, that the Father may be glorified in the Son.*

There have been numerous times when I have felt something just "come over me." Depression. Discouragement. Anger, lust, fear— coming out of nowhere, and for no apparent reason. I have learned that these spirits may be trailing me, or I may have just passed through a nest of them. Whatever, they are attaching themselves to me and traveling right along with me. I used to bring them home from the prisons where I ministered, before I was taught about them. I have learned to recognize that feeling of something "not quite right." Any strong emotion or desire that suddenly and unexpectedly appears, you can guess it might be a spirit. And you have the authority to cast if off. "Get out of here, you spirit, in the name of Jesus Christ."

If you like exciting reading, let me recommend the book of Acts. Read through it and see all the things wrought by the hand of ordinary apostles and saints. It will inspire you!

A Special Word to Ladies

Everything said in this book about men applies to you, also—God loves you! And it is His desire that you be delivered. When I began writing this book, I did not know any struggling ladies personally. There seemed to be far more men than women strugglers. Since beginning the book, however, a number of ladies have come to me about their desires and their pain, and crying out, how can they be delivered! (Maybe that spirit is sitting on my shoulder as I type, but I believe that it is God drawing people to a willing vessel so He can help them.)

A lady, not knowing about this book and my ministry to homosexuals, came to me and began to speak about her pain. She had been serving God for almost 30 years, had never backslid, had always been faithful, to the church and to God. She explained that there were some strongholds in her life that she was not able to tear down. She said she had not acted on them, but that they were tearing her apart—all she could think about was this obsession—and she could think of no other word to describe it. Her obsession, she said, was lesbianism.

She waited for her confession to sink in. I merely nodded and said, "I know that." She continued to explain that this obsession consumed her—day and night—asleep or awake. She desired women.

You wonder, how can that be? Instead of answering that, let me tell you that there are more of our sisters than you might ever dream who are struggling with sexual desires for women. Like this woman, most of them have not been acted upon. The problem is, however, if God does not intervene pretty soon, it is only a matter of time before our dear sisters weaken and give in.

This sister later asked me, how did I know? I explained that there was a spirit attaching itself to her, and that I recognized the spirit. She said that lesbians everywhere were attracted to her—why? Because, they, too recognized that spirit. In addition, the more attached the spirit becomes to a person, the more that person can take on the "appearance of the homosexual." The men look more effeminate, the ladies more masculine.

One lady told me she thought she was gay because she did not like ladies' books, like romance novels. I said, Well hallelujah, I am glad. I told her I did not like them, either, and that I taught against romance novels, and I am not a lesbian. I explained that I was so busy in my Father's Kingdom, when would I find time for those things? She, too, was busy in the work of the Lord. She was a lady of purpose, a lady who prayed and knew the mind of the Lord. She moved with determination and vision. She was often criticized by the men for what they called "lack of femininity."

There are different kinds of femininity. There is the delicate lace around the throat (that chokes the life out of me), and there is the relationship with the Lover of my soul—a relationship with my Creator, who made me just as I am. He did not put all the extra weight on me, but He did give me my high cheekbones, which some have called masculine. He gave me my personality, my preferences. These are from my Lord, and have nothing to do with homosexuality. No one makes me feel more "feminine" than Jesus!

I wear jackets and blazers most of the time. I'm lost without pockets, especially when I'm ministering. I need a handy place for my Kleenex and Altoids and ball point pen. I have had several ladies lament that they hate carrying purses. I hate bothering with them, too, but I have such a fondness for them that my husband calls me the "bag lady." There is nothing wrong with liking pockets. If you feel this means you are a lesbian, look back over your life to where this lie began. If you study your life along with this book, you will probably begin to see a clear pattern.

There are some things that can be changed. A manly gait? Ladies, we can train ourselves to walk differently. Most of us just need to slow down some. I usually have a strong, fast stride, leaving people far behind—even my husband. I am half way across the store when he calls out, "Babe, come look at this!" And I have to stop and retrace my steps. Why, I wonder, don't I just slow down and keep pace with him? We have discussed it; I am fast, he is slow. That has nothing to do with our sexual "orientation."

Again, it comes to the relationship we have with Jesus. The more we know Him—the better we know Him—the closer we grow to Him—the more protected we will feel, the more feminine. This is a heart attitude that will bleed over into everything we do.

Soon you will adding a curl or two to your hairstyle. Maybe a soft scarf across your shoulder. Just tiny touches. I believe these little things are pleasing to the Lord. I believe that He delights in His ladies!

9

How to Minister to the Homosexual

I was thinking about that pastor who once said that he would welcome gays—if they cleaned up their act first. Nello, if I had had to clean up my act before coming to God, I never would have made it! This is not to imply that we are to allow unrepentant homosexuals to run rampant in our churches. This cannot be. But we have to realize that some things take time.

There are people do not want to spend a lot of time on homosexuals because some of them will return to their former lifestyles. So what?—there will be MIAs from *all* lifestyles; being heterosexual does not guarantee we won't lose out with God. One preacher said this: "I can win 25 heterosexuals in the same amount of time it takes to win one homosexual." I responded to that preacher with this: "If that *one* were my boy Stephen—to me, it would be more than worth it all!" As Brother Doty says, "Jesus left the 99 and went after that one." But, besides all that, I think a lack of patience can result in some of that disappointment. We need to have commitment to these people—and they need to have commitment to change.

When you step out and begin to minister to this population, remember—first of all, prayer. Pray for God to lead you to a soul. Pray for wisdom and love and understanding. Pray for the anointing. The most important thing you can do to reach the homosexual is pray. Prayer will tell you when to go and when to stay away...when to speak and when to remain silent. And prayer will help you overcome all the fears you may have in reaching out to them.

Hopefully, by the time you get to this chapter, you will know the first thing that you *don't* do is badger the homosexual. You do not dump condemnation upon his head. If the Lord is actually drawing a person, fear not—they will hear. For the person who is not yet being drawn, who still has a hardened mind and heart, then it makes no difference how many volumes of consequences we present, they still won't hear. We can always plant a lot of seeds, and then God will take it from there, but it just seems to me that when God opens a door, why not share His hope and love and His perfect way to freedom.

As you begin to minister, you will notice some little quirks—which is actually baggage the homosexual has picked up over the years and is still lugging around. Nello and I want to try to help you understand this person. Following are some things you may find yourself facing with the souls God sends to you:

You will encounter deception. Because of the life they have lived, and the damage it has done, they will be bringing with them rebellion, and they will lie to cover up mistakes. Confront them with their lies. They are so afraid of not being able to make it, and of not living up to the expectations of others. They might not like to admit it, but they very much want to please others—you!

You will encounter strong fears of rejection...sometimes a lack of hope, a "what's the use" attitude. Fear that others will suspect them, or even accuse them of coming on to them. Because of this fear, they will sometimes appear to be snobbish when, in fact, they are just afraid of getting close to other people, especially other males in the church. They have so many fears, connected with a loss of identity..... Think about it, they are going to be walking away from life as they have known it.... leaving all of their friends, social life, possibly a partner, possibly their job, you name it, they will be giving up everything. Talk about walking into the unknown! And just as difficult, entering a brand new life, new people, new friends, the church, that's all brand new, and they have to start all over. There is also the fear that they will have to live the rest of their lives alone.

Stephen told me just recently: "Where I am now, I am with people who grew up very similar, if not identical, to me. I just feel like I *belong*."

Yes, Stephen, I can see that there could be a special sense of connectedness, a sense of belonging, a sense of being understood in a world that can't really understand.... And when you don't have the words to explain, there is no need for the words.... everybody understands.... for some of it, there are no words..... only feelings you can't explain .... But, Stephen, you can have all of that, and so much more, with Jesus. Just because you did not experience this fully when you served Him before, does not mean you cannot have it now. You are a different man, in a different time and place. The time is right. And my prayers for you now are very different.

That sense of belonging! And then to think about leaving the "safety" of all that.....leaving the people who understand you .... and to go into a strange and hostile world.... Do you see, Church, what our competition is like? Do you see the work that is cut out for us? But we can do it! We can do exploits! There is not a doubt in my mind—because I know God (Daniel 11:32)!

We need to help them to achieve the feeling of belonging in the church—and they do belong. They belong to Jesus, and they belong to the family of God. MIAs, especially, can never belong in the world. The world will never truly understand them. But God does! God is the only one who can understand us. What a thrill it is for me, personally, because I have always seemed to march to a different drumbeat. Very rarely have I had the privilege of "belonging." But God knows me, and understands me, and I belong to Him.

A Ministry to the Homosexual?

As you begin to step out in ministry to this special group of people, you will find yourself dealing with three specific groups: First, look around you. There are those that are still in church, but suffering. We cannot know the many tears they might cry in the solitude of their homes. We have no idea how many times they have cried out to God, begging Him to remove these desires and take away this awful confusion! My heart is especially heavy for this group, because Stephen was once here. If only someone had reached out to him then!

One thing I've noticed is that we have a program, an outreach, for just about every sin there is, except one. We have no ministry for the homosexual. A youth came to me last year and asked if I could refer him to someone who might help. I personally knew a number of people who had been delivered from the homosexual lifestyle and were now serving God and doing a good job of it, but they were not willing to confess it publicly.

If we can just manage to get past our personal feelings, we would see young people who are confused, lonely, and hurting. They are being bombarded on all sides by the homosexual agenda. Many are in the stages of questioning, seeking, and looking for answers. If we cannot provide them, Satan will be sure to send someone along peddling his lies, eager to deceive our people. And we will lose them. And then sit back and cluck and say, "I knew it all along."

There are more Apostolic people than we realize struggling with this issue. I believe that if we could just reach them, and let them open up and talk about their fears and hurts, we might be able to rescue them.

The Missing in Action

Next are the MIAs... Stephen now fits in this category. He has moved from the first group into this one. These are the ones who found no one to talk to, and could not resolve their questions. These are the ones who have already drifted into the lifestyle and want out. They have tried it, they have learned, the hard way, that things are much better in the Church. But they are so deeply involved, they just don't know how to escape. I talked with such a young man personally. He really did touch me. "I don't blame anybody," he said. "I don't blame the church, and I don't blame Mom and Dad. I used to sit at that piano dying inside. I knew something was wrong inside of me and I didn't know what. I began to read. I read a lot of stuff on being gay. And the more I read, the more it seemed to fit. This was a nightmare, because I knew that, as a Christian, I couldn't go into that kind of thing. And yet, I didn't want to be alone for the rest of my life. I would sit there, playing for the choir, and dying inside."

"Did you ever talk to a counselor?" I asked naively.

"I did. He's the one who pushed me over, because he told me I needed to go ahead and get it out of my system, that I'd never have peace until I did."

I choked, I really did. "Why didn't you seek out a Christian counselor?"

"That *was* a Christian counselor. My pastor recommended him."

Both of us were at a loss for words now. After a minute, he went on. "I finally just gave up. And now I want out. It's bad out here, it really is."

"Why don't you come back?"

His eyes glistened with unshed tears. I saw his pain, it was all over him. "I don't know how. I don't feel much hope anywhere. I don't know how to get out of this thing, it's like a spiral. I just don't know how to get out of it." If he just had someone—a true Apostolic—who had been in this, and then got out—if he could just talk to someone like that...!

I have learned since that day that there are men who have been delivered, and are willing to step out and talk about it. They are few and far between. This is why Nello is so precious to me. I wish there were more like him. And David says, "Almost two years ago God did a marvelous thing...He delivered me from the homosexual lifestyle after fifteen long years. Being able to deal with all the hurt and pain and coming to understand and learning how to grow and let God have control has been a true blessing."

The third group is those who do not know the Lord at all. We have to lead them to salvation. Acts 1:8 gives them the key: *"And ye shall receive power after that the Holy Ghost is come upon you."* We need this power resident in us in order to overcome anything. We need to lead them to the Lord.

No one is saying it will be an easy ministry; it will not. It is vital that we have a strong prayer life, because we will be coming against spirits. You will find yourself praying against specific spirits that refuse to let go. You will find yourself in some kind of "deliverance" ministry—maybe even wondering what you are doing there. It is spiritual warfare, and we have to be willing to pay the price. But if we are—we can pray until *any* spirit is broken!

Beacon Ministries has such a ministry in the Lighthouse United Pentecostal Church of Cape Cod. It is my desire that every church have some kind of outreach to the homosexual. Sometime my heart gets so heavy for these lost people, that I long to take to the streets and hold them and love them to Jesus.

The Pleasures of Sin

NELLO: I think one of the hardest things for the church to realize and to accept is that, at first especially, what we have to offer is not nearly as thrilling and electrifying as what the homosexual has experienced. Their life has been one whirl of chaos and confusion. There was always a party going on, another bridge to cross over, and a new conquest. For a long time, there was always something exciting happening. Never a dull moment. When the pain began to be felt, it had to be squelched at all costs. Rather than dealing with the pain, it was masked by another stage of denial or another new drug or partner. Drown out the pain, at all costs—pretend it isn't there!

LAD: So don't go trying to tell the homosexual that he has not felt pleasure in his sin. Even the Bible tells us that sin has its pleasures. Our aim should be to lead the homosexual to the same conclusion as Moses. Hebrews 11:24 tells us: "By faith Moses, when he was come to years, refused to be called the son of Pharaoh's daughter; Choosing rather to suffer affliction with the people of God, than to enjoy the pleasures of sin for a season."

Help them to come up higher. Help them reach a place where they have a Cause! Help them discover a meaning for life, a reason for living! Something to live for, something to die for! Help them to come outside themselves by looking up and looking out! Give them a vision! Without a vision, the people perish. We have to have something bigger than ourselves, or we will die.

I know many, many people who live alone and will probably never marry, and they have learned it is not the worst thing there is. After my first husband left, I lived alone for almost 25 years. There were some pretty rocky places, and a lot of loneliness. But I did reach the place in God where I was working for a higher cause. My life was a fulfilling one, because my vision had changed. We need to have a vision and be able to impart it to the gay person. The longer one lives the homosexual life, the narrower their vision becomes.

So we see that the first thing we must have, for ourselves and for others, is a vision. *Without a vision, the people perish (Proverbs 29:18).* What are some other things the church can do, Nello?

NELLO: Let's face it, when it comes to pleasing the flesh, the church can't even come close to what the gay life has to offer the flesh. Boredom is a huge issue. What the church has got to make available to replace the "pleasures of sin" is a *true* sense of warmth, love, family, closeness. We have got to physically touch them, give a pat on the back, put an arm around their shoulder..... Don't be afraid to make contact.... Nothing is going to rub off, you won't catch anything. And for the individual, this is very difficult for them to do because of their fear that any contact will be interpreted as a come-on. Sharing has got to be more than just surface stuff. In sharing and talking with the individual, share some of your own shortcomings, problems, things that the Lord helped you with, brought you out of.

When I first began my struggle out, God sent Shawn to me. The kind of sharing I just mentioned was one of the biggest things that helped me initially to build my trust with Shawn. He's the first contact that I had with the church, and he stood by me every step of the way, but I did not trust him at first. I remember him telling me about when he had orange hair, and we won't even go into the body piercings. But that sharing made him "real" to me, and I could relate. All of a sudden I was not talking with a holy, holy, holy saint, but with a real human being who had been delivered from sin. That I could relate to and that's what I wanted.

And homosexuality needs to be discussed openly without the individual feeling that they will be put down or judged. They need to know and feel that they truly are included and are a vital part of the church family. Fake stuff won't work. At the right time, have them active in some church work, ministry, endeavor... very important. See what they have to offer to the church, what kinds of gifts and talents, and then use them. Most of these people are exceptionally talented.

Invite them over for dinner. This is especially good for them because it helps them to get to know people in a smaller setting, and helps to break down distrust. All of these things will take time, so watch out for expecting them to receive the Holy Ghost one night and be a perfect saint by the next service. Patience, lots of patience, and some "extra" attention for a short period of time..... But don't just then drop all of it at one time. For them, it's sort of like being a foreigner, traveling to a strange, new land where they know no one, don't know any of the customs.

LAD: A lot of us don't have patience, Nello—and especially that kind of patience.

NELLO: You know what I say to that? We'd better start getting some patience. Are we going to sit by and watch people go to hell because we aren't willing to work on ourselves? The Bible does say, *"In your patience possess ye your souls"* (Luke 21:19). Sounds pretty serious to me.

Something else: This may sound trivial, but please, learn to say the word "homosexual" without turning red and getting embarrassed. I have met Christians who can't even speak the word.... I actually had one person spell it out.... and that's the truth.

The individual has got to get grounded in the truth. Small group studies—some one-on-one with people who can be counted on to be there for them. Sometimes it's more important to just be a listener and you don't always have to give them an answer, or advice. Just listen.

Working with an individual who has spent years in homosexuality is not going to be a "one night job"..... It's planted, and rooted deep. I remember Shawn telling me that he had been praying for the Lord to send him a soul to win.... and that what he had in mind was a "neat little Bible study" ... perhaps a couple of Bible studies, then to the altar, and then smooth sailing. And he said to me, "Look at what the Lord sent me!" We still laugh about that one.

Keep in mind that for a church of any size, more than likely, there are going to be other members struggling with these feelings but who have been too fearful to reach out for help. So when you have someone come in, and stand up and testify about homosexuality, there are going to be some other things that will start happening in the church. So be aware..... And prepared to minister to, and to be a support to those who start to stand up and reach out.

Why Revival Tarries

LAD: Wow, I am thinking about something—just imagine if all our churches had this kind of revelation and visibility—people standing up in testimony services telling how God had delivered them from this particular sin. Word would spread, folks would lose their fears, gays would be free to come into our churches, shame and all, knowing they would be met with understanding and with love—and patience. Oh! I love to think of it! You know what else—it would spell "early church revival" because it would mean the Church has reached a whole new level!

We keep praying for revival. And yet are we really *prepared* for revival? What I mean by that is that we have churches full of babies and the emotionally wounded. So what happens when all these new babies and emotionally wounded flood our altars in revival? I feel very strongly that our attitude towards homosexuality can be a very real barometer of our readiness for revival. If we feel that we would rather see these souls in hell than have them in our churches—I honestly cannot believe that God will grant us revival. Think about it.

Confront with Love

NELLO: Sister Doty, keep in mind also that things can happen that will be misunderstood, even when the church members are doing their very best to help and make the person feel comfortable. Remember that the gay person brings with them a lot of shame, distrust, and fear.... so remember that it's going to take time for healing. But with time, as the Lord gives them new understanding, it will happen. I know.

Now all of this does not mean that we side step or ignore the truth.... the new person must indeed hear the truth, there will be times that they will need to be "confronted," have things explained to them, we are not talking about letting things slide. But, as with all sin and sinners—sharing the truth, teaching them, correcting them—must be done with God's genuine love! We do not compromise anything.... but there are two ways to disciple them.... one way is of the Lord; the other is not.

The Issue of Fear

LAD: There are many reasons saints fail to reach out to those struggling with homosexuality, and the biggest one, I think, is fear. Nello, you won't believe this—no, you probably will—I have actually seen a saint get up and sit on the other side of the church when she learned that someone on her pew had AIDS. (I have seen it happen with a cancer patient, also, so I know it is a very real problem.)

NELLO: Oh, yes, I almost forgot about some in the church having a fear of getting AIDS. Yikes, this is a biggie. There is a lot of false information out there about AIDS and there needs to be some education for church members about it. The bottom line is that they aren't going to catch AIDS, and it's also important to remember that just because a person is gay does not mean that he has AIDS. The majority of gays do *not* have AIDS.

Another big fear is that, if they get around a gay person, the gay person may make a pass at them. They believe that all that gay people want to do is have sex, and they believe that the gay person doesn't care who they have sex with, just as long as it's the same gender.

LAD: Well....from what I've heard, and seen in the news, that's pretty well true, isn't it? Some of their rallies and parades are worse than the New Orleans Mardi Gras.

NELLO: What you just said...*the news*. Sister Doty, you know how biased the media are. Gays, in general, can be just as selective as heterosexuals when it comes to who they get involved with. Think back to when you were dating....some guys you liked, some you didn't... Well, gays are the same way. They have the same feelings, likes, and dislikes, when it comes to a partner.

LAD: Nello, I also happen to know about their clubs and bars and bath houses…. Some people think women don't know anything about what goes on—especially Christian women. But since Stephen left, I have studied this subject extensively.

NELLO: I know you have. And there are those out there who do head to the club with one thing on their mind and they end up with anybody who will have them. And if alcohol and other drugs are introduced into the picture, they will also end up with someone that they normally would not. But this is not just a "gay thing" … I guarantee you, walk into a heterosexual singles bar, or a bar in general, and see what you find. You'll find the same thing. Now that does not make any of this okay, because it is all sin…. but what I'm saying is that just because a person is gay does not mean that they want to get involved sexually with you. The chances are good that they are not even interested in you that way.

And to take this one step further, the opposite is probably truer—many gays would actually distance themselves from you, out of a fear that you might think they are interested in you. Very few, if they were attracted to you, would ever make the first advance. And again, I'm aware that there is always the exception.

LAD: Nello, I hesitate even to ask you this question, but there will be people who want to know….in this kind of ministry…what if—just what if?—a gay actually did make a pass at them? What should they do?

NELLO: I guess I would ask the question, what would they do if someone of the opposite sex made a pass? Well, basically, the same thing would apply here. The problem we encounter here is that fear factor…. it's treated like it's something totally different … fear sets in, the person being come on to feels their own sexuality threatened, they fear there is something about them that is "gay" and is causing the attraction. They think that a different response is needed, lash out, protect their masculinity, if we're dealing with males. The truth is, simply say, "Thanks, but no thanks, I'm not interested; that's not why we are here, that's not what we are here to discuss." And then, what if the person did not stop, well, what would they do if it was the opposite sex and they would not stop? Simply say good-bye and leave. It really is that simple.

Another point is that if you are working with a person and you see that they seriously want the Lord, it could be possible that they might actually develop an attraction for you. If that should happen, it's important for them to be able to be open, and talk about it..... That's not the same as "coming on" ... the gay person has to learn how to relate to the same sex. To them, most anytime they felt attracted, it was just *assumed* that it was a sexual attraction, or, that's the only way they were able to "connect" to another person. Now they are learning that they can have feelings of love and attraction and that that does *not* mean that it's sexual..... So, if the person reaching out is aware of this, and if the gay person is able to share if they do feel "sexually" attracted, this can actually be a real step of trust, a real breakthrough, and then they can pray and work on that issue.

But, the bottom line to your questions is to Just Say No. I would venture to say that if the Lord is drawing that person, and if they are in fact serious, that's never going to happen. Even if they were attracted, they would not act on it.

Also, when meeting to talk, until you know the person, and know that they are really serious, always make it in a busy, public place, like a restaurant. And after getting to know them, and if they come to church with you and are able to perhaps meet one other person, then you can always meet as a group of three, and that would make it easier to meet in a home.

A Personal Experience

LAD: Nello, you just mentioned being able to talk about the attraction. That is very important, and I'll tell you why. I remember one time, many moons ago now, when I was attracted to my lady flight instructor. (It is not unusual for ladies to get "crushes" on other ladies. We do not speak of them, because most of us do not understand that it is normal, and are fearful of being labeled lesbian.) We spent many hours alone together in the airplane. She was older than I, settled in her ways, solid. I fancied I was "in love" with her and spent a lot of time rehearsing how and when I was going to tell her.

One day we went to the airport coffee shop and, sitting face to face, I revealed my feelings. I did not know if she might reciprocate—

or slap me—or laugh at me. As it turned out, she did neither. She listened carefully. She kept eye contact as I spoke. Then she let me know up front that she did not have those kinds of feelings—for me, or any other lady. We discussed this, and she actually helped me to understand that I was still searching for a mother's love. I still needed the comfort, nurturance, and acceptance of *me* for being me. If I could actually tell another woman I loved her and not have her reject me, it would mean so much. You see, I struggled with feelings of mother-rejection all my life. I did not want to have a sexual relationship with the flight instructor. But that was the only feeling I knew to equate with it. We need to talk to our young girls, and let them know these things are normal—otherwise, they could end up eventually drifting into lesbianism.

So I know how important it is to be able to talk through our feelings about someone. Once I did that, my friendship with this woman became just that again: friendship. With the deep hunger for a mother's love, it would have been an easy thing for me to drift into a lesbian lifestyle. I suppose that is why I can so easily understand a man's hunger for a father's love, and how it can develop into homosexuality.

It is also why I know that, if a homosexual can only learn to relate to other men as men and not as father replacements, they will soon know deliverance. As long as there is a suspicion of sexual innuendoes, there will be a holding back...a reluctance to allow a heterosexual man to get close. And the irony of it is that this is just what is needed: warmth and closeness. Closeness as brethren. Closeness as family.   Freedom to be me and still be accepted. Receiving and giving love and realizing it has nothing to do with sex, but everything to do with fulfillment.

Jesus said to call no man Father. Sometimes we use that in reference to certain churches. But I believe we also need to understand that in God as our Father, we find all nurturance...all fulfillment...all peace, joy and love. We can rest in His arms as a child. We can know safety, maybe for the first time in our lives. God is not an earthly father. I don't care how good your daddy was, or how bad...how saintly, or how mean. No daddy can compare with God when it comes to being a Father! He is all good, all caring. He assures us in His Word in Jeremiah 29:11: *"For I know the thoughts that I think toward you, saith the LORD, thoughts of peace, and not of evil, to give you an expected end. "*

When Jesus walked on this earth, He met all types of people. He responded to all kinds of problems and hurts. He knew and understood pain. Many times His eyes would look upon the multitudes with compassion. And He knew that the human creature needed a true Father relationship, and so He taught us about that aspect of God.

John the Beloved

When John the Beloved laid his head on Jesus' bosom, it was not a sexual thing. It was a nurturing thing, a trusting thing, a giving-and-receiving thing. John loved, and was allowed to love. It would have been an easy thing for Jesus to nudge John to sit up and "act right." And the other disciples could easily have made fun of John, but, like the woman with the alabaster box, he did not care. He was willing to risk all for love.

Jonathan and David

The love between Jonathan and David is one that homosexuals everywhere claim was a homosexual relationship. But those who claim this are the very ones who have no clue how real men relate to other men. Scripture tells us that David had seven brothers, and that he was the youngest. Only the imagination can tell us how this was for David, but one thing we can safely surmise: David learned how to relate to males! He was familiar with them. David was not lacking in male relationship.

And that is why he felt safe in loving Jonathan—not because he was desirous of his friend sexually—but because he knew the meaning of man-to-man love. After Jonathan's death, David mourned his best friend whom he loved as his own soul. He said, "I am distressed for thee, my brother Jonathan: very pleasant hast thou been unto me: thy love to me was wonderful, passing the love of women." David had many wives and concubines whom he also loved and who bore him children. The great love of his life among women was Bathsheba. But David also recognized and appreciated that love between men is not the same as that between a man and a woman. It is not better; it is not superior; it is just *different.*

Oh, that homosexual men everywhere could learn this lesson! Oh, that they might experience the freedom, as did John, as did David, to give and receive love from another man, not even thinking that someone might look askew upon it. I believe one reason that God put this friendship in the Bible is to give our men a model.

Oh but Sister Doty, David and Jonathan kissed! Now, what do you say about that!

I say this: that the same man, the apostle Paul, who wrote I Corinthians 6:9-11, and Romans Chapter 1, is the same man who also wrote four times in the New Testament, to greet each other with a holy kiss. The brethren kissed each other, and it was not a nasty thing, as we think of it today, in our culture; but it was a holy thing.

And we women share holy kisses. I often do it. A lady in the church, who is my adopted daughter, frequently kisses me on the cheek. And I have seen the brethren kiss. My husband tells me he has kissed a couple of the brothers. When I read this particular section to him, he made a face and said, very emphatically: "Believe you me, there is nothing at all sexual when I kiss a brother!" (And I definitely believe him!)

Until I settled the mother deficiency in my own life, I was not able to love other women as I do today. I was afraid. I was afraid that it was a sexual thing, even though it was not. And so I held back, remaining in my love-starved condition. Today I can say that I love women, and I know—and other women know—that I am not speaking sexually. It is lovely, and it is rewarding to everybody concerned.

What is Deliverance?

We have been talking about the gradual healing of homosexuality. There is also another kind—albeit, especially in reference to this particular sin, rarer—and that is instant deliverance. Just as God can heal our physical bodies on the spot, so can He deliver one from awful sin. I would never dissuade one from asking God for an instant deliverance, because I know God, and God can do anything He wants to do. We do know that deliverance is His will for us, because He would not have any of us to live in sin. There is a scripture that is so very precious to me. I John 5:14-15: *"And this is the confidence that we have in him, that, if we ask any thing according to his will, he heareth us: And if we know that he hear us, whatsoever we ask, we know that we have the petitions that we desired of him."*

Many people are afraid of deliverance because of some abuses and misuses of it. I have been in churches where they use buckets every service—and it seemed to me like the same people were getting "delivered" in service after service. I do not see that in the Bible. Spirits often "tare" people when they came out at the command of Jesus, and I have seen them do the same today. But I do not see Jesus running for a bucket, and I do not see the same deliverance being repeated over and over. Once Jesus did it—it was done. And I believe that is how it should be today. Listen to this account in Matthew 17: 14-21

> And when they were come to the multitude, there came to him a certain man, kneeling down to him, and saying, Lord, have mercy on my son: for he is a lunatic, and sore vexed: for ofttimes he falleth into the fire, and oft into the water. And I brought him to thy disciples, and they could not cure him. Then Jesus answered and said, O faithless and perverse generation, how long shall I be with you? how long shall I suffer you? bring him hither to me. And Jesus rebuked the devil; and he departed out of him: and the child was cured from that very hour. Then came the disciples to Jesus apart, and said, Why could not we cast him out? And Jesus said unto them, Because of your unbelief: for verily I say unto you, If ye have faith as a grain of mustard seed, ye shall say unto this mountain, Remove hence to yonder place; and it shall remove; and nothing shall be impossible unto you. Howbeit this kind goeth not out but by prayer and fasting.

Perhaps the disciples—because of their lack of faith—all piled onto the poor boy whose father was seeking deliverance for him. But again, I do not see Jesus sitting on anybody and holding them down while He chatted with the devil. Small wonder so many of our people are fearful of what they have come to know as "deliverance."

However, I have seen people delivered so many times I could not begin to count them. Melinda describes being delivered from lesbianism upon coming up out of the waters of baptism:

> It was the most incredible feeling I had felt in my whole life. I felt totally cleansed, like a new creature. My homosexual desire, alcoholic desire, and every other sinful desire was left in that water. God had washed me with the blood of His Son. There is power in the name of Jesus !!! Everything was completely different after that. I did not realize how my life would be completely transformed. I had totally new desires and feelings. I was so excited that I wanted to tell everyone about Jesus!

I myself was delivered from many things. At the very hour that I received the Holy Ghost sitting on that tree stump in the wilderness, I was delivered from alcohol. It would have been wonderful had God seen fit to deliver me of cigarettes just as fast, but He did not. He took another avenue with me in that area.

When I received the Holy Ghost I was smoking four packs of strong cigarettes a day—and had already been under conviction for almost a year. I had tried everything to quit—lettuce cigarettes, filters, gum and candy, behavior modification, hypnosis—and nothing had worked. I was so ashamed of my weakness—especially after receiving the Holy Ghost—that I banished myself from the house when I smoked. I was preaching the love of God wherever I went, and sometimes I would have to close a service too soon because of needing a cigarette. And all the time living under self-condemnation.

How to Stop Smoking (or Anything Else)

One day the Lord instructed me to get a new composition notebook and my Bible, and start reading. Every time I came to a scripture that quickened me, I was to write it down in the notebook. I was to write out the entire scripture; not just the reference. I did not understand why, but I knew to obey the Lord. Soon I had a book nearly full of scriptures, and that was when the Lord spoke to me about my smoking.

He said He was not going to ask me to quit smoking, but that every time I wanted to smoke, I was to first sit down and read all the scriptures in my notebook—then I could go smoke.

Initially, I raced through the scriptures because of craving the cigarette, but soon I began to slow down and actually enjoy what I was reading. It was the Word of God, and it was doing something strangely beautiful inside of me!

Finally on the third day, I sat down to read before smoking, and lost all desire to smoke. God delivered me. He took away all desire for cigarettes! God be praised! That is deliverance! Total deliverance from all desire to smoke—to drink—to do the things I used to do! God is a good and awesome God!

He could have delivered me instantly of cigarettes, the way He did of alcohol, but for some reason, known only to God, He chose to do it another way. I do know that a number of people I have shared this with have found the method very helpful—not only for cigarettes, but for other addictions, as well. Not all deliverances and healing in the Bible were instant—one man was told to go dip in the River Jordan. In Mark 8, one man's blindness was healed, but not completely until the second time—the first time he saw men "walking as trees."

There may be someone reading this, and desiring deliverance from homosexuality, and asking God to remove all desire. God can do that. Just recently a lady came up to me at a conference. She did not know about this book, or my burden for homosexuality. She just began talking: "I just have to tell you that all of my life I was a lesbian, Sister Doty. I always did the 'boy part.' I had several long-term relationships with women, and loved them as much as I could, but I was always so angry inside. I stayed angry all the time, and so empty. God finally brought me to [this city] and led me to the church here. When He filled me with the Holy Ghost, He took away all of my desires for women. And I mean ALL of them! In all these years of serving God, I have not wanted to return to live that way. And now—these past couple of years—I have felt a loneliness for a husband that I have never felt. I pray that the Lord will send me a husband, for that is now my heart's desire."

This sister, like so many others, was totally, instantly delivered. God can do the same for you—but He might not, at least not for awhile. So don't be discouraged if he doesn't. Sometimes God asks something of us first. Sometimes He wants to see if we really mean business; He will test us. Sometimes He wants us to step out on faith,

100

exercising that faith. Sometimes He asks things of us that will help us grow stronger spiritually. The point is, you can be an overcomer, and still have some battles to fight. Do not allow the enemy of your soul to lie to you at this crucial time! After you have surrendered to the Lord—been born again, or returned to Him—things will probably go well at first. You'll be excited and "on fire" for God. You'll feel like you can lick the world! It's euphoria! You have faith for anything and everything. If you think about the future at all, it is with confidence and assurance that life will always be this wonderful! And then...your balloon bursts.

Perhaps it is a temptation to slip back into your old lifestyle. And because you had the temptation, you begin to condemn yourself. "That's awful! I should *never* think things like that—ever again!" But the truth of the matter is: you *did* think it. And this is where the devil comes in. He will resume his lies to you. He will accuse you of all kinds of ungodliness. This point is very critical, dear one! Do not listen to him! Get in the Word and do as Jesus did—fight the devil with the Word of God! Memorize scriptures and spit them out into the atmosphere. Walk through your house, reading the Word aloud. Fill the environment with His Word!

You *are* an overcomer! You have left the sinful lifestyle, and you have given your heart to God. You are still standing, even though the enemy has been trying to destroy you. You are still hanging in there. Joel 3:10 says to let the weak say, I am strong. This is not being a hypocrite; it is feeding your soul with the Word of God. The Word of God is true. And guess what—you have a *BIG* God! Nothing is too hard for Him! Hang onto Him—the two of you can do great things!

10
Can Gays Really Change?

I get so tired of people saying that homosexuals cannot change. Don't limit God that way! If Christians could only realize what they are saying when they say that—they are saying that our God is limited in what He can do. And I am here to tell you, I have a God who can do anything! Nothing is too hard for my God! If your god is so weak and powerless that he has to leave these poor hurting souls in their sin—I suggest strongly that you come to know the God that I serve. His name is Jesus, and there are no limits on my Lord!

Homosexuals can change! I know too many who have! I have studied too many testimonials, too many lives, not to see the evidence. Paul confirmed it two thousand years ago when he said, "...and such were some of you." Paul knew there were people in the early church who had been deeply embroiled in the homosexual life. Did he condemn them? No. He was thankful for them—because he knew God had done it. He outlined the process in the next few verses, where he spoke of sanctification, justification, the power of the Name, and the Spirit of our God.

"And such were some of you: but ye are washed, but ye are sanctified, but ye are justified in the name of the Lord Jesus, and by the Spirit of our God" (1 Corinthians 6:11). Notice that it says, "and such *were* some of you." It does not say, "and such *are* some of you." Some of the Corinthian believers had been homosexual, it was common back then (and some of them had been drunkards, adulterers). But they had changed. They had been homosexual in the past, but after they met Jesus, they no longer were. They had had an encounter that they would never forget! They were homosexual no longer. When they met the Master, and fell in love with Him, their desires changed. No longer did they want the old; now they were new creatures. Now they were, in today's terminology, ex-gays. This gives great hope to every homosexual or lesbian because it is proof that a person can change. By the grace of God such a person can be justified (declared righteous in Christ), sanctified (set apart for God's service) and washed (judicially cleansed of all sin). *"Therefore if any man be in Christ, he is a new creature: old things are passed away; behold, all things are become new" (2 Corinthians 5:17).*

Positive Steps to Change

1. Honestly admit that homosexuality if wrong and is a sin.
2. Determine in your heart that you will stop the behavior.
3. Seek—and accept—help from others.
4. Put away all lying.
5. Get your focus off of yourself and onto God and others.

Perhaps the greatest mistake that an individual who wants to overcome homosexual desires can make is to focus on changing his or her desires—such a focus is a set up for failure. To focus constantly on changing one's desires is to focus on self. Nowhere in the Word of God are we admonished to focus on the self and the sin that so easily entangles us. Rather than asking God to immediately change their desires, the Christian should seek to develop a strong, consistent relationship with the Lord. The nearer one draws to God, the more His character develops in the person. Over time ungodly desires will fade; sinful behavior will become less appealing as one begins to see it from God's perspective rather than from their own.

In would be unfair to promise any individual that all temptation will be taken away; it may not. As long as we remain in these mortal bodies we will do battle with the sinful flesh. However, we can find great encouragement even in times of struggle. In 2 Corinthians 4:16-18 we read: *"For which cause we faint not; but though our outward man perish, yet the inward man is renewed day by day. For our light affliction, which is but for a moment, worketh for us a far more exceeding and eternal weight of glory; While we look not at the things which are seen, but at the things which are not seen: for the things which are seen are temporal; but the things which are not seen are eternal."*

There is an abundance of pro-homosexual literature stealing all hope from desperate people by claiming that they cannot change—that maybe they can regulate, or control, their behavior, but they will always be enslaved to homosexual desires. This is what they say. And it is "politically correct." Gay activists are infuriated with people who change. They say they are "narrow-minded" for even desiring to change. When one stops and thinks about it, however, they are the ones being narrow-minded.

Minister Freed from Homosexuality

Here is part of a testimony from a minister of the gospel. Hear in his own words what the Lord has done for him:

"[When my wife found out]... she chose not to leave me, and in desperation she sought out help from an Exodus referral ministry. For the first time I heard that I was not alone, there were others who had walked out of homosexuality to find change, freedom and fulfillment. Lies I had for so long believed were seen as the fiction that they were. The truth had been there all along but I had failed to see or hear it. In my early Christian walk my zeal for what truth I had received, prompted me to pursue ministry. The ministry would soon replace intimacy with Father God as I worked to fix myself and fill the hole. Service would become the enemy of relationship. I felt that the first step would be to get all the things I had been stuffing into the hole out, so that God could fill it appropriately. I left the ministry and the pulpit for a time to heal and learn. I made myself accountable to my pastor and a few other men that knew all about my struggle with homosexuality. This time of disclosure was terrifying for I had no idea how people and peers would respond. The response was overwhelmingly positive. I began realizing that people loved me not for what I did, but unconditionally as I was. I began building healthy same sex relationships with heterosexual men as the Holy Spirit weaned me off of my gay friends and the gay community. Jesus was so patient as I gradually said good-bye to my past and all that had become a part of my secret identity. The many safe men in my life began confirming my masculinity and my identity in Jesus. For the first time I had friends that I trusted and felt close to, I had nothing to hide. I could be real at last! I found an intimacy in the body of Christ that would help to heal the wounds of the past. I found an intimacy with Christ that I had never known, and with this intimacy came gradual change as the hole began to close. I am still learning and healing. Every day the freedom and hope grows as I find my true identity in my Heavenly father. To many that have known me the change is obvious.

"I share where I've been, with the prayer that it will bring hope and freedom to you. You too can find freedom from homosexuality and other sexual sins. Freedom is not a process, or a seven step plan but a Person; that Person is Jesus Christ. Perhaps you know Him already. I challenge you to seek Him out, lay hold on Him and know Him as never before. He is Truth. The Truth will set you free!"

But What Does The Research Say?

Colin Cook, Co-Founder of Homosexuals Anonymous: "No matter how deep your homosexual feelings are, deeper still, buried under all the confusion and feelings and habits, lies your heterosexuality."

I know that gays can change. I know people who once were that way and no longer are. They have wives and children and are happy and well-adjusted. And I have heard many testimonies of those who have changed. But what do the professionals say? The researchers? One of the most exciting days for gay activists was when the American Psychiatric Association deleted homosexuality from the diagnostic manual in 1973. No longer was it considered a "disease" that warranted treatment. Now it was considered something that could not be treated—thus it could not be changed. That was a giant step forward to its acceptance as an "alternative lifestyle."

Now, however, the psychiatrist who led the team that instigated this change, says homosexuality *can* be changed! Dr. Robert L. Spitzer, Professor of Psychiatry and Chief of Biometrics at Columbia University, did a new study that drew worldwide media attention in 2001.

"Like most psychiatrists," says Dr. Spitzer, "I thought that homosexual behavior could be resisted, but that no one could really change their sexual orientation. I now believe that's untrue—some people can and do change." He reported interviewing 200 subjects (143 men and 57 women) who were willing to describe their sexual and emotional histories, including their self-reported shift from gay to straight.

Don't Tell *Us* We Can't Change!

Most mental health associations argue against the ex-gay ministries. They believe that homosexual fantasies and feelings can be stuffed down or resisted, but not transformed. At one time, Dr. Spitzer agreed, but at the American Psychiatric Association's annual conference in 1999, he was drawn to a group of ex-gays staging a demonstration at the entrance to the conference building. The picketers were objecting to the APA's recent resolution discouraging therapy to change homosexuality to heterosexuality. They carried placards saying, "Homosexuals *Can* Change—We Did—Ask *Us!*" Others said, "Don't Affirm Me into a Lifestyle that was Killing Me Physically and Spiritually," and "The APA Has Betrayed America with Politically Correct Science.

Some of the psychiatrists tore up the literature handed out to them by the protesters. But others stopped to offer the protestors a few quiet words of encouragement. Dr. Spitzer was skeptical, but he decided to find out for himself if sexual orientation was changeable. Better late than never, I suppose. But many people either have not heard of his new study, or refuse to believe it.   It was a significant study. He developed a 45-minute telephone interview which he personally administered to all the subjects. Most had been referred to him by The National Association of Research and Therapy of Homosexuality and by Exodus, a ministry for homosexual strugglers.

To be eligible for the study, the subjects had to experience a significant shift from homosexual to heterosexual attraction which had lasted for at least five years.

Most of the subjects said their religious faith was very important in their lives, and about three-quarters of the men and half of the women had been heterosexually married by the time of the study. Most had sought change because a gay lifestyle had been emotionally unsatisfying. Many had been disturbed by promiscuity, stormy relationships, a conflict with their religious values, and the desire to be (or to stay) heterosexually married.

Be Patient! Don't Give Up!

In the study just cited, the effort to change typically did not produce significant results for the first two years. Subjects said they were helped by examining their family and childhood experiences, and understanding how those factors might have contributed to their gender identity and sexual orientation. Same-sex mentoring relationships, behavior-therapy techniques and group therapy were also mentioned as particularly helpful. To the researchers' surprise, good heterosexual functioning was reportedly achieved by 67% of the men who had rarely or never felt any opposite-sex attraction before the change process. Nearly all the subjects said they now feel more masculine (in the case of men) or more feminine (women).

"Contrary to conventional wisdom," Spitzer concluded, "some highly motivated individuals, using a variety of change efforts, can make substantial change in multiple indicators of sexual orientation, and achieve good heterosexual functioning." He added that change from homosexual to heterosexual is not usually a matter of "either/or," but exists on a continuum—that is, a diminishing of homosexuality and an expansion of heterosexual potential that is exhibited in widely varying degrees."

This study is believed to be the most detailed investigation of sexual orientation change to date. The assessment tool was developed with the assistance of a New York psychiatrist, and used a structured interview so that others could know exactly what questions were asked, and what response choices were offered to the subjects. The full data file is now available to other researchers, including tape-recordings of about a third of the interviews, which (with the subjects' permission and without any reference to their names) can be listened to by investigators who wish to carry such research further. "[Homosexuals] should have the right," Spitzer stated, "to explore their heterosexual potential."

(The above material was adapted from the website of the National Association of Research and Therapy of Homosexuality (NARTH www.narth.com,, by Linda Ames Nicolosi.)

There are also numerous autobiographical reports from men and women who once believed themselves to be unchangeably bound by same-sex attractions and behaviors. Many of these men and women now describe themselves as free of same-sex attraction, fantasy, and behavior. (Exodus North America, 1990-2000, Update. Exodus: Seattle WA) Most of these individuals found freedom through participation in religion based support groups, although some also had recourse to therapists.

Unfortunately, a number of influential persons and professional groups ignore this evidence. (American Psychiatric Association, 1997, Fact Sheet: Homosexuality and Bisexuality. Washington DC: APA. September, and Herek, G.,1991, "Myths about sexual orientation: A lawyer's guide to social science research." Law & Sexuality. 1: 133 -

172.), and there seems to be a concerted effort on the part of "homosexual apologists" to deny the effectiveness of treatment of same-sex attraction or claim that such treatment is harmful.

Barnhouse found this absolutely amazing: "The distortion of reality inherent in the denials by homosexual apologists that the condition is curable is so immense that one wonders what motivates it." (Barnhouse, R., 1977 Homosexuality: A Symbolic Confusion. NY: Seabury Press.)

Jeffrey Satinover, MD and Ph.D., has written of his extensive experience with patients experiencing same-sex attraction:

"I have been extraordinarily fortunate to have met many people who have emerged from the gay life. When I see the personal difficulties they have squarely faced, the sheer courage they have displayed not only in facing these difficulties but also in confronting a culture that uses every possible means to deny the validity of their values, goals, and experiences, I truly stand back in wonder... It is these people -- former homosexuals and those who are still struggling, all across America and aboard -- who stand for me as a model of everything good and possible in a world that takes the human heart, and the God of that heart, seriously. In my various explorations within the worlds of psychoanalysis, psychotherapy, and psychiatry, I have simply never before seen such profound healing." (Satinover, J., 1996 Homosexuality and the Politics of Truth. Grand Rapids MI: Baker.)

The above material was obtained from a paper presented on the website of www.narth.com: HOMOSEXUALITY AND HOPE: Statement Of The Catholic Medical Association, November, 2000.

11
Overcoming, Growing, Changing Process

We come to the Lord just as we are.... We make our way to the altar of repentance just as we are....We repent, we are baptized in Jesus Name, and the Lord will fill us with His Spirit, we will receive the Holy Ghost, evidenced by the speaking of other tongues. And, as wonderful as the new birth experience is, it is just the start of our journey..... That gives us our ticket to get onboard God's train, heading down the tracks to spend eternity with Him. Now our job is to enjoy the ride, and make sure that we don't take any detours along the way!

NELLO: We must make a total, clean break from our past. And that means everything—people, places, and things. Not easy, but certainly not impossible.... I know that for a fact, and I know that I'm not the only one who has made this kind of break. The old friends have to go, the old hangouts, the old things—all must be cleaned out. And when I talk about cleaning house, I'm including the actual cleaning of our homes. You will not believe how many 30-gallon trash bags of "sin" I packed out of my house. And with some of that stuff, it was like my flesh was being torn away. And, truly, it was—an actual dying OF the flesh.

We must dive in, head first, to the things of the Lord..... Prayer, reading our Bibles, fasting, church, our church family, more prayer and fasting.... Now by saying that, I am not giving the usual pat answer; I am not saying, "Just go and pray about it, just go and read your Bible." I am speaking of absolute commitment—a life steeped in these things. They must become entwined with our lives, part of their very fabric. If only more Christians everywhere could get a hold of this kind of consecration—what revival we would have!

When you go to church, you are there to worship your God, not to be concerned about what others are thinking or doing. God and his work must be your number one focus and your number one priority. MIAs—you were probably never this dedicated before in your walk with God. You are in for a new walk, an excitement you have never experienced before. You will actually be *living* for your God! God and

His work will become your burning desire and top priority. Nothing else can compare with this!

Now just a note here.... if all of this does not happen the day you receive the Holy Ghost, don't worry. The key is to *never, never, never* give up, never stop getting back up. It helps so much to keep your focus on your goal of freedom. Try not to look at the inconvenience, the hurt, the frustration of the circumstances today—keep your eyes on the path up ahead. I have a scripture for you here: Romans 8:18 *"For I reckon that the sufferings of this present time are not worthy to be compared with the glory which shall be revealed in us."*

Again, the Lord knows our heart, and it might take some time to shed more of the old; we think we have let go of everything only to find another part that we are still holding on to. But as long as we keep moving forward, no matter how slow it might seem, then we will arrive at where the Lord wants us. Patience is a hard thing for most people, but with gays, I'm convinced it's extra hard. They have learned to please the flesh as quick and easy and as often as they want. And now they must wait upon the Lord and deny the flesh. The point is, the Lord is the only answer, and your focus must be on Him as our answer and our hope. And watch out.... the "miracles" will begin happening.

We must learn to be open about our past.... believe me—anything that we keep secret will eventually be used by the enemy against us—and most gays became the masters of deceit....having to hide who we were, having to hide the life that we lived ...And all of that deceit causes fear, shame, and anxiety, and pushes us away from others. The enemy loves secrets. But the moment we share the truth with others, the power of the secret is broken. It can't be used against us any more. We don't have to worry if we are telling the same story the same way ... we don't have to fear that what we share with one person might get to another person ..... Once we are able to say Lord, this is Yours; You take care of it....Wow! What freedom. And it's then that we are able to truly have the support, the understanding, the love, the openness, and the closeness to other people that we want, and need so very much.

This Thing About Marriage

People are always asking the individual who has come out of homosexuality, "So, when are you going to get married?" It's like getting married is the "proof" that the person is no longer gay. There has been pressure put on homosexuals and heterosexuals alike, to get married..... Once they get to a certain age, it's almost like a requirement. I'm not sure how it is with women, but if a guy is not married by a certain age, gossip starts. Some people go ahead and get married, just to get people off of their backs. People who struggle with homosexuality often use marriage in an attempt to prevent anyone from digging too deep. And it's only a matter of time until the marriage is in trouble.

LAD: Nello, I deal with these wounded wives on a consistent basis. The devastation will tear you apart to see it. They don't know what to do—wait for the husband's deliverance and return—get a divorce and move on with life? And children compound the problem—it's far from easy.

NELLO: I know, Sister Doty. And for the individual who has been in the struggle and then come to the Lord, they too start trying to "fix" the situation and think that if they get married, everything will just go away. As we come out of homosexuality, our first and foremost goal needs to be building a strong and close relationship with Jesus. We must not make it our goal to "prove" that we are now heterosexual. But sometimes that takes us a while to realize, and until we do, we can get ourselves into some big trouble. I think that's why it's so important that our pastors and our churches are aware of this, too, and be there to guide the individual in building that relationship with the Lord first rather than using marriage to change them from homosexual to heterosexual.

LAD: That is the Lord's work, and I've seen Him do it over and over. I know of people who once were deep into homosexuality but are now married and leading content and productive lives as fathers and husbands—wives and mothers. But these people did not rush it. They allowed healing to take place at the Lord's pace—in His perfect timing. This takes patience, and in the microwave society in which we live, we want everything—yesterday. But if we will just force ourselves to slow down, and wait on God, it will be absolutely worth it all!

One thing I really believe is that God does not want us to merely survive in this world; He wants us to be complete, whole. And in most cases, that means having a husband or wife to share your life with. Some people truly are called to celibacy and with that gift, can live happy and complete lives; but if they do not have that particular calling, I believe God can and will restore heterosexuality to their lives. You see, Nello, God is our Creator. That means He can create something out of nothing. There is nothing God can't do, and restoring sexuality to a life is nothing for Him. The frigid heterosexual wife...the impotent heterosexual husband...God can repair whatever went wrong so they can enjoy intimate relations with their spouses. And if God can do that, He can restore any homosexual to wholeness, make them alive and complete, and fulfill His will in their lives.

NELLO: Wow, Sister Doty! I agree, it's up to the Lord to determine who will get married, and who will remain single. This all goes back to "seek ye first the Kingdom of God and then..." Some people will get married and have kids, while others will live a life where their entire energy is going to be on the work of the Lord. That takes dedication, but God can really use people like that!

Coming out of homosexuality left us alienated from everything; from ourselves, from others, from God.... I don't think that we ever knew what "love" really was, and I know that we didn't have a clue about God's pure love.... everything about love was so distorted, so based on lust, and now as we come to the Lord, it really takes time to allow the Lord to teach us His real and pure love. And it will be His love, which, if we are to get married, will lead us to the mate that He has planned for us.

For myself, if the Lord sends me a wife, I know that it will not be based on sexual lust. I believe that if it happens, I will fall in love with that lady, based on who *she* is, on her inner beauties, on her walk with the Lord, on her love, and then after marriage, according to God's plan, the Lord will take care of everything else. So I just don't worry about it any more. I just say, "Lord, Your will be done." Either way, I now have the most important thing, I now have the only thing that I really need, and that is Jesus Christ!

Let's go back a second to the "Seek ye first..." Sometimes, those coming out of homosexuality are their own worst enemies. They will focus solely on their issue of homosexuality.... And they are not able to see anything else or do any of the other things that the Lord wants them to do. They are so busy looking for the "exact answers," the "exact causes," (and there's nothing wrong with wanting some of those answers, even though we probably won't ever have all of them), but they stay so busy on that one issue they end up getting stuck there. And then they get discouraged that nothing is happening, that nothing is really changing. We have to start working for the Lord, serving Him in the ways that He calls us, *before* we have become *"perfect!"*

Do We Now Desire A Woman?

Listen to this question: "So now that you are no longer homosexual, do you want to be intimate with a woman?" You cannot believe how many people want this as the proof that an individual is no longer involved in homosexuality. If you don't become a "ladies man," then there must still be some problems. And to take it a step further, I have actually had "saints" from the church (not my local church) say that if we have lust toward a woman, well, that's OK because that kind of lust is "natural" and "normal"—thus, okay!

You were talking about deliverance, Sister Doty, and I know that the Lord can do *anything* instantly if He so desires. And I'm sort of inclined to believe that when we receive the Holy Ghost we are in fact delivered from homosexuality. But then we find ourselves in the battle against our flesh, and we get confused and start feeling that we have not been delivered, after all. What happens is, memories will come, and now we must make some new choices; we must choose to resist. And I know for a fact that, as we continue standing fast with the Lord, all of that old stuff does decrease, does happen less and less often....

LAD: I encourage everybody—please—just wait it out! Listen—let me give you something that will help: here are four "magic" words that will get you through every situation, every time: *This too shall pass.* And another thing—do not go by your feelings! They will steer you wrong. The Bible says to walk by faith and not by sight. Feelings can steer us wrong every time. Stick to the Word, to what you know is true.

There will be times that old thoughts do pop into your head, but heterosexuals also have temptations and struggle with their thoughts. There will always be temptation, and we will always have to fight in this battle against the flesh. Jesus Himself was tempted, but did not sin. Those old ways of thinking have got to be brought under control, have got to be "cast down," as Paul said. But you see, here is where the enemy can trip you up: he will tell you these thoughts and temptations are because God has failed, and you have failed, and you are *still* homosexual. He will cause you to forget that all of us fight similar things! Homosexuals and heterosexuals alike will battle things like lust, but the enemy of your soul will try to hide that fact from you. Here is another scripture for you: *"There hath no temptation taken you but such as is common to man: but God is faithful, who will not suffer you to be tempted above that ye are able; but will with the temptation also make a way to escape, that ye may be able to bear it."* I Corinthians 10:13

Prescription: Spiritual Vitamins!

NELLO: What helps me is what I call my "spiritual vitamins" which, when taken in large quantities, build up my resistance to attack by the carnal virus! The more I'm praying and fasting and in the Word.... the less that The Old comes to mind, the fewer the temptations, the less often and with less intensity. Also, remembering to "seek ye first the Kingdom of God and then" .... if my eyes are on the Lord, if my focus is on the Lord, letting Him do the fixing, not me worrying about it, not me trying to fix me, but saying I'm serving the Lord no matter what— serving and loving with a made-up mind!

Our Testimony

Revelation 12:11—that's my scripture.... *"...and they overcame him by the blood of the lamb and by the word of their testimony..."* I've made a commitment to testify every chance I get, and that I'll testify at every church service..... No matter what I feel like, no matter if all I do is stand up and say Praise the Lord. I'm stomping the enemy in the face with every testimony I utter! It also helps me resist temptation during the week, between services....It's hard to give in to temptation and then stand up and testify for the Lord. This is powerful.

114

Accountability

An accountability partner is a potent tool in helping us to resist temptations. Get one as soon as you can, but make sure you take the time to find someone you can really trust, and feel comfortable with. You will actually be sharing every week what you have and have not done..... It's a great way to have support and prayer, and it's also a powerful tool to resist temptations during the week—knowing you will have to be confessing it to somebody in a few days. It could prove to be embarrassing—but make up your mind that you will be honest!

Renew Your Mind

LAD: Remember that when you are born again, you become a new creature—but your mind has not necessarily been renewed yet. You will have to learn a whole new way of thinking. Don't allow the ugly, defeatist thoughts—refuse them. Cast them away. In their place, dwell on the beautiful things of God. Memorize scripture for those times when you need a new thought—fast. Paul knew this to be true when he wrote II Corinthians 10:5: *"Casting down imaginations, and every high thing that exalteth itself against the knowledge of God, and bringing into captivity every thought to the obedience of Christ."*

Paul also give us an awesome prescription in Philippians 4:8: *"...whatsoever things are true, whatsoever things are honest, whatsoever things are just, whatsoever things are pure, whatsoever things are lovely, whatsoever things are of good report; if there be any virtue, and if there be any praise, think on these things."*

No boredom there! It seems to me that, if the homosexual can just get the right perspective here, and learn to look upon all of this as simply the challenge that it truly is—they will make it.

Make Up Your Mind

NELLO: It *is* a challenge! But you see, Sister Doty, I have done it, and I know it can be done. And I know it is a small price to pay for this delirious freedom that I now walk in! We must reach that point where we finally say "OK God, I give up, I want *out!*" We must make that choice for ourselves, and then take the risk of reaching out for help. The Lord will open the doors; He will lead us to a pastor and a church that will be safe, that He has prepared for us.

As we start this journey out of homosexuality, we really must remember to "Seek ye first the Kingdom of God, and *then*..." Remember, we don't have to be "fixed" first.... Only God can fix a broken human being. Our job, our responsibility is to just seek the Lord, to work on building that close and personal relationship with Him and by doing so, He will then do all the fixing that needs to be done. What a relief, what a load off of *our* shoulders to know that we don't have to do the fixing, we just give ourselves to the Lord..... Talk about being in good hands!

Get Back Up!

We must also determine to get back up! No matter how long it takes, no matter how many times we slip, stumble, or make mistakes; no matter what anyone else says, no matter what, we must repent and get right back up and continue moving forward with our Lord. That's what He's there for; we must choose not to listen to the lies of our flesh and the enemy, but rebuke those things and get right back into the hands of our Lord.

Keep Your Past Dead

If we don't continue to "kill" our past, whatever we allow to remain of our old life will sooner or later raise its ugly head and be used against us. I've had to learn that the hard way. We must also continue to remind ourselves that our old sin was no worse, was not bigger, than any other sin and that the Lord we serve is big enough, powerful enough, to deliver us from *anything*. Don't listen to the lies of the enemy when he comes saying that we can't make it, when he says that homosexuality is the exception to what our Lord can take care of ..... That's a big fat *lie*! And never, never stop taking your "spiritual vitamins."

Use Your Support System

As Sister Doty said earlier, when we reach the point that we just can't pray any more, PRAY MORE. Don't forget support ... we must have the support, the love and guidance of our Pastor, of our brothers and sisters in the Church. We cannot carry a secret around.... the shame will pull us under.... in God's time, we really need to open up, get all of the past out in the open and in doing so, we receive the help, the support, the love from others, and the shame, the enemy, is defeated. And through it all, remember that perseverance is the key. Keep on keeping on! Never turn back, no matter what.

Forgive, and Accept Forgiveness....

12

The Issue of Forgiveness

I am going to wrap something up in this final chapter that can truly set you free, and help you to stay free, and walk joyfully in your new deliverance. I want to head you off at the pass from making a mistake that can spell doom to your continued victory in Jesus.

The fundamental energy of psychology and the self-help industry is the emphasis on *self*, and this preoccupation is not biblical. For example, while scriptures teach that we are to esteem others better than ourselves, our psychological goals revolve around improving the way we look at ourselves. This training of the human being to search within himself for happiness and fulfillment has ushered in tremendous pain and regret. By way of example, one specific area is the psychological industry's injunction to "forgive yourself."

That is what this final chapter is about—how to forgive those who have hurt you...and to settle the issue of so-called "self-forgiveness," so that you can truly walk in new and lasting freedom.

Some people just cannot seem to "keep the victory." I don't want you to be one of those. The same problems surface over and over again. Just as they begin to make progress, they fall back again. They seem to live under some generalized sense of guilt. Their past will not remain past. In numerous cases like this we hear them saying: "I just can't forgive myself." And so they (once again) fall into condemnation, and (once again) lapse into a major depression and/or their old sin, and the cycle starts over again. As we work with these unfortunate and hurting people, we try to lead them into the forgiving of self. "God has forgiven you," we cry, "and so you must forgive yourself." If they can ever get past the point of self-recrimination, we think, they'll finally have it behind them. And so we assign a misdiagnosis, if you will, that can be more hurtful than helpful.

Many of these hapless souls are eventually referred out to the friendly, neighborhood psychologist. I mean, after all, we really want the best for our people; so even though we experience a pang of guilt, we figure we've done all we can. We breathe a sigh of relief and await the good report of healing. But, alas, it never comes, and soon we are hearing again the old refrain, "But I just can't forgive myself!"

119

We wonder where we go wrong, when all the time, we are swimming against the tide of biblical truths—biblical truths that teach us that if we seek to save our life we will lose it, but if we lose our life for His sake, we save it. To the psychologically minded, this is "mumbo-jumbo." Indeed.

Robert Jones says in *The Journal of Pastoral Practice* (10.4): "But has [the client] identified her real problem? Or has she become stuck in one particularly unpleasant symptom of an as-yet-unidentified root problem? Is self-forgiveness the solution? Or is there a deeper solution to a deeper problem?" He goes on to point out that the Bible speaks not one word about forgiving oneself. It speaks of vertical forgiveness (God forgiving us), and horizontal forgiveness (when we forgive others). But we are nowhere instructed in internal forgiveness.

I once believed all of this myself, and I was wrong. I shudder to think back to the days when I imparted this erroneous teaching to hurting souls, because I realize now that I might have done more harm than good. And so I have had to repent and go on from there, with thankfulness that God had given me a deeper understanding. It is all right to be wrong; it is not all right to continue in wrongdoing when God reveals the truth.

I have come to realize that trying to lead someone down the road towards the forgiving of self is like placing a sentence upon a person without the possibility of parole. It can set a soul upon a path of pursuing a nonexistent goal that is impossible to realize. And even sadder, is the fact that, while we keep the focus on self-forgiveness, the true cause—the root problem—is being neglected.

Homosexuals, especially, often try for years to forgive themselves, and continually fail. They are failing because they are attempting the impossible. Forgiving oneself is not a biblical principle. They are trying to do something God has never asked them to do.

What is really happening is that somehow these people short circuit, and are unable to accept and apply God's forgiveness to their lives. Eventually, because of this false teaching and trying to accomplish the impossible, they just give up. They no longer seek healing, but resign themselves to a fictional version of "bearing their cross"—or, worse, they become MIAs.

The gist of the problem rests in the modern concept of victimization. As a society, we have bought into the victim mentality hook, line, and sinker. No one is guilty of anything any more, because everyone is a victim of someone, or something, and therefore cannot help what they do. The wife abuser is not guilty—not really—because he learned the behavior from *his* father. The teenager who shoots and kills three of his classmates did not mean to do it—not really—it's just that he has been so mistreated. The terrorist bomber finds sympathy, because he "never had the opportunity to develop socially and emotionally (no mention of spiritually)."

So along comes the psychologist who tells us that the victim must save himself—an impossible goal. The Bible tells us that man is guilty, and cannot possibly save himself. He has to have a Savior.

I personally sought for many years to forgive myself for the way I raised my children. As an alcoholic mother, one can only imagine some of the hurt I must have inflicted upon my little ones. Many were the nights I wept into my pillow, thinking about then the harm I must have caused. How well I recall one particular night in the prayer room. I was crying out to God with heartbreaking sobs, when a brother came alongside to try to help. He told me these words that night: "Sister, you've got to forgive yourself. If you don't, you'll never make it."

He meant well. He was trying to help, but it was as though he had passed sentence on me. We all mean well. We truly care about the hurting, and long to reach out with healing balm. But repeating psychobabble is not the way to help.

But the Lord is faithful, and He led me to the liberating truth that I was only a sinner saved by His grace. Nothing more. Nothing less. He forgave my past. He forgave the things I did to my children. And then for me to stand up and say, "I can't forgive myself," only brought grief to a caring, giving God.

Breakdowns in Receiving God's Forgiveness

As I began to pour over Bible biographies of very wicked men who were recipients of the grace of God, I began to understand and receive His forgiveness for my own wicked life. As this happened, I came to realize the problem had never been an inability to forgive myself—it was an inability to accept the fact that God had truly cared enough, about *me*, to forgive *me*. I have later learned this is the most common reason for the failure to "forgive oneself."

Again going to The Journal of Pastoral Practice, we learn that there are a host of possible points at which a believer may experience a breakdown in properly receiving God's forgiveness. Perhaps the person has failed to see his sin as a direct offense against God. David, in his memorable psalm of repentance, cried out, *"Against thee and thee only have I sinned..."* (51:4). This is a very common condition in today's world where sin is no longer called sin. After all, why should one confess a "disease" and repent of it?

Too often, we view God as someone to pal around with on Sunday morning. This kind of God, we reason, does not see us as grievous sinners, but as kids who have been abused and mistreated and so He "understands" why we do the things we do—so why confess and repent?

Another view of God is that of a small, very limited God. We have tucked Him away in a box; therefore we fail to grasp just how *big* He really is. Only a *big* God can forgive the worst kinds of sinners (and on a deep level, we know that's *us*, even though we use all the euphemisms to deny it). And since He's "not big enough" to forgive the worst, we fail accept His forgiveness.

We learn to view our own sins as bigger than God and His grace. To lead one, therefore, to seek self-forgiveness, not only pilots them toward an unobtainable goal, it fortifies them in the sin of pride. Proverbs 16:5 warns, *"Everyone that is proud in heart is an abomination to the Lord...."*

We can believe God has not forgiven us because we are continuing in the same old sins. When we do not grow spiritually, but remain weak and carnal, it will not be long before we resort to the old sins of which we were forgiven. J.R. Ensey explains, "He repeats the same sin because, in terms of growth, he is the same person. His stunted sanctification results in repeated defeat at the hands of this besetting sin. And his ongoing 'inability to forgive himself' is a veiled surrender to its binding power." (Ensey, Christian Counseling from Scripture)

And so we sin, and at first we seek forgiveness. But after we have been forgiven time and time again for the same sin, we are soon too ashamed to go back to our loving Father. We turn our faces away—much like Adam and Eve when they heard God calling in the cool of the day.

Perfectionists are demanding of themselves—often placing strict and rigid demands on their time and work and lifestyle that God does not require. The result is that they fail to live up to their own standards of perfection. Robert Jones says, "His longing for self-forgiveness arises from his failure to measure up to his own standards of performance, his own image of how good he is or ought to be."

We can begin to see how keeping the focus upon self, and continually looking within, will dwarf our vision and twist our thinking. The failure to "forgive oneself" is, as a result of this self-centeredness, actually rooted in pride. Martin and Deidre Bobgan state, "Confessing our sin to God and to one another and then receiving forgiveness from God and one another should result in humility and gratitude. Not receiving and believing God's forgiveness, either by not confessing sin or by holding onto a self-righteousness that says, 'I can't forgive myself,' is prideful and ungrateful. It places one's own evaluation over God's...." (Bobgan: *"James Dobson Believes In Forgiving Self, But..."*) www.psychoheresy-aware.org

Instead of striving, then, for an impossible goal, work instead on your relationship with the One Who loves you more than His life itself. Striving to forgive yourself will keep you away from the realization of who He is; while coming to know Him will satisfy that longing in your soul. As Nello says, "Seek ye first...."

Forgiving Others

The Bible speaks of only two kinds of forgiveness: forgiveness by God, extended to us; and forgiveness by us, extended to others. God's mandate to forgive those who hurt us is, thankfully, not based on feeling. We are told to walk by faith, not by sight. Another way of saying that is that we are not to depend on our feelings but upon what the Word of God says. Since the Word says we must forgive, we know it is an attainable goal whether we feel like it or not. We must choose forgiveness or unforgiveness. It is our choice to do one or the other.

Neither does forgiveness depend on forgetting. If your husband leaves you for someone else, you can forgive him—but you cannot forget that he left, because he is no longer there. When the kids ask, "Where is Daddy?" you do not say, "Uh....who is Daddy?" God does not wipe our minds clean; to "forget" means to never hold it against that person again. You will remember it, but it no longer dominates your life. You will not bring it up again.

I have heard this: "I will forgive him just as soon as he asks me to." That does not work. We must forgive whether or not he ever asks. This is between us and God—it is a salvation issue. When Jesus cried from the cross, "Father, forgive them...!" it certainly was not because his tormenters had repented. He left us an example.

Sometimes we have to forgive the same person many times. We do a good job of forgiving and believe it was thorough. Then we find out there is still something lurking that must be dealt with. As we grow and mature, we reach higher levels, and experience new issues. They may require fresh forgiveness.

Many people ask me if forgiveness requires that we reconcile with that person. It is desirable if we can. But sometimes the pain is just too great for reconciliation to take place. I worked with a young woman once whose father had sexually abused her over a period of years. As she and I began the counseling experience, the father offered to pay for her sessions. This looked like a positive sign that father and daughter were reconciling. After a couple of sessions, however, I discovered what was really happening. The father was demanding that she come to his office before every session to ask for the money. Once there, he made her beg for it. He was abusing her all over again!

I went to visit him and requested that he send me a check at the beginning of the month. As I was leaving my business card, he told me he refused to do that. If she wanted him to pay, she would have to come pick it up.

I continued the sessions with her, but without compensation. Reconciliation was not possible because he had never repented of his sins.

But I Have Tried—and Cannot Forgive!

Almost without fail, "cannot" means "will not." But once in awhile, it may be true, when it involves a hurt that has escalated into bitterness and has actually become enmeshed with the spirit. It is similar to the nature of sin that we discussed in Chapter Four. Prayer and fasting can break this, but only if we have a strong desire on our part. This is where many of us fail: we do not have the desire to let the other person off the hook.

Remember the chapter that discussed your desires as they related to coming out of homosexuality? Remember, we determined that you cannot change your own desires. But first there must be the decision—a choice of our own stubborn self-will. As we go to God in prayer and fasting, we learn that we must wait upon Him. At this point, there will be very little emotion.

But as we continue to wait on God, and He sees that we have purposed that—with His help—we are determined to forgive that person, we will slowly begin to feel some desire. Like Elijah, after the seventh time, when he saw the tiny cloud, like a man's hand. Sometimes things do not come so easy, and we live in a microwave world where we want everything fast and effortless.

Forgiving is usually a process. We are in a state of "forgiving." It comes gradually. This is a key, because if we insist on having it instantly, we will probably give up before we attain it. Learn to wait! As we wait on God, we will begin to feel a release, and we know that something is working within us. That will be the spirit—or gift—of forgiveness, without which we will never be able to fully forgive the other person.

Oh dear one! Will we never learn that we are nothing in and of ourselves?—and that we can do nothing in and of ourselves? He told us so clearly that we are mere branches. He is the Vine, and from the vine flows all of life.

Let's purpose in our hearts to please God. Let us make that our life's goal. And when we do, we will have a strong desire burning within us to do those things that are pleasing to Him—and that includes the difficult things like denying ourselves...carrying our cross...and forgiving others. It will become a joy!

A Parting Word

And so we come to the end of this journey together. With all of my heart, I yearn for your deliverance. With all of my heart, I want to see you saved. I would like to leave you with this thought, that you let your first goal in life be to make Him smile. Learn to live for that smile! Learn to live to please *Him!* Dote on *Him*—enjoy *Him*—relax in *Him,* and let Him be the captain of your soul. I love you so much—but even more important—so does *He!*

"...The Beginning...."

FAVORITE SEMINARS

Maximum Victory

A biblical approach to the problems facing the church today, as well as a program for their prevention. *Maximum Victory* should follow all New Converts' training. An excellent 12-week course. *Maximum Victory*, with its 12 "Power Steps" has been used to satisfy some court and probation requirements.

Lynda Allison Doty's understanding, wisdom, and teaching will cut to the core. Her no-nonsense approach, mixed with humor and real-life scenarios, make reaching your maximum potential an awesome, enjoyable journey. You *can* change! You *can* be the person God created you to be. Follow these "Power Steps to an Awesome Life."

The Power of God Thinking

A concentrated course to get people on the right track to godly thinking. The Bible says to cast down imaginations, and every high thing that exalteth itself against the knowledge of God, and bringing into captivity every thought to the obedience of Christ. Discover the POWER that results from a life of godly thinking!

Lynda Allison Doty
PO Box 292100 ~ Sacramento, CA 95829
www.awpministries.org
Director@awpministries.org ~ ladawp@aol.com

NELLO POZZOBON was born in Arizona, and grew up in Missouri. At the age of 20, Nello entered the U.S. Navy, and spent six years traveling over the world. He did his undergraduate work at Southwest Missouri State University, then on to his Master's degree in Social Work, Columbia University, New York City. Brother Pozzobon worked as a psychotherapist at Rutgers University, before moving to Cape Cod, Massachusetts in 1991, where he served as director of a community mental health agency.

When he made his way back to the Lord, Nello left the secular field. He is now in private practice, moving into Apostolic Counseling. He is founder/director of Beacon Ministries, and is preparing for full-time ministry. He presently attends The Lighthouse of Cape Cod United Pentecostal Church. Nello works with people on the internet, by e-mail, telephone, and letters. You may contact Brother Nello at:

Beacon Ministries
5 Deerpath Circle ~ Brewster, MA 02631
1-888-580-2661
www.beaconministries.net
beaconministries@aol.com

LYNDA ALLISON DOTY speaks widely throughout the country, teaching others how to apply the concepts of biblical counseling, both in their own lives and the lives of others. Her work is epitomized in her most recent book, *Maximum Victory*, where she leads others, through the Word of God, to realize their potential in Jesus.

Sister Doty is married to a minister who shares her burden for the hurting. They currently minister out of Sacramento, California, and are part of The Rock Church, Nathaniel J. Wilson, pastor, where Brother Doty serves on the pastoral staff. Sister Doty is an instructor at College at the Rock, and teaches counseling by correspondence and in local churches. She also serves on the Board of Directors of the Institute of Soteric Counseling, which is headquartered in Sacramento, California.

Lynda Allison Doty
PO Box 292100 ~ Sacramento, CA 95829
www.awpministries.org
Director@awpministries.org ~ ladawp@aol.com

Books & Tapes by Lynda Allison Doty

Gay Conversations.............$8.00
Maximum Victory...............9.00
Walking in Trust................7.00
Apostolic Counseling 9.00
Help Me Heal..................10.00
Lord, Why Am I Crying?........9.00
Lisa Said No....................12.00
Larissa's Song..................14.00
Goodbye, Granny Dix...........8.00

Tapes
Depression! (2-Tape Set).....12.00
Lord, Break Me!......................5.00
Spiritual Warfare................5.00

Books by Deborah Randall
On Spiritual Warfare
Treasures of Darkness.........10.25
Being Expert in War.............11.25

Send check or money order, along
With your name and mailing address,
Plus 18% postage
To:

Lynda Allison Doty
PO Box 292100
Sacramento, CA 95829